D1566133

Presented to

Pleasant Valley Ch. Library

In Memory of

mother of Esther Morri

By

Judy & Ivan Cate

NEXT YEAR IN JERUSALEM

לְשָׁנָה הַבָּאָה בִּירוּשָׁלַיִם:

NEXT YEAR IN JERUSALEM

Walter K. Price

moody press
chicago

To
G. P. Comer
who helps me remember
the glories of the sawdust trail

ISBN: 0-8024-5928-5

Library of Congress Catalog Card No.: 74-15341

All scripture quotations in this book are from the American Standard Version, 1901. The name *Jehovah* has been changed to "the LORD" or "GOD."

Printed in the United States of America

CONTENTS

PREFACE

ADDRESSING AN ASSEMBLY in Madison Square Garden on the occasion of Israel's third anniversary, Abba Eban summarized the new nation's achievements. Said he, "Here is a people which defended its life, its home and its open gates against the fury of a powerful foe; set up an oasis of democracy, liberty and progress in a wilderness of despotism and squalor extending in vast expanse on every side; received into its shelter 600,000 of its kinsmen coming out of the depth of insecurity and want; multiplied the centers of settlement and cultivation beyond any scale hitherto conceived; began to explore and uncover the hidden resources of its soil which had lain neglected for centuries; caused water to gush forth in the most primeval wilderness of recorded time; extended the foundations of its industrial progress; embarked upon one of the great cultural adventures of history, to create out of diverse and remote citizens a unified society in the tongue and the spirit of Israel's past; established its banner in the family of nations and gave utterance to Israel's immemorial yearning for world peace. All this the people of Israel, sustained by Jews throughout the world, have accomplished within this brief span of time. Is this not a convincing proof of the courage and vitality, the resilience, the spiritual vigor, the capacities of self-sacrifice which repose in the people of Israel and the Jewish communities throughout the world."

Twenty-two years later, in 1973, Israel celebrated her twenty-fifth anniversary. What Dr. Eban said on her third anniversary is even more true today. The courage and vitality, the resilience, the spiritual vigor, the capacities of self-sacrifice which repose in the people of Israel have been validated far more today than was apparent when he spoke in 1951.

However, while we are convinced of Dr. Eban's basic premise that Israel has made spectacular progress during the

7

last twenty-five years, the thesis of this book utterly rejects Eban's inference that the achievements of the new nation Israel are due solely to the Jews' own initiative and achievement. Israel in the land has demonstrated great courage, vitality, resilience and spiritual vigor; however, the incentive is of divine origin, we believe, and not due solely to the idealism and enthusiasms of the Jewish community, either in Israel or worldwide. We view the new State of Israel as the most prophetically significant event of the last two thousand years. It represents the initial fulfillment of a mass of Bible prophecy which has declared that the people of Israel will return to the land before the second coming of Christ. The twentieth century—from the First Zionist Congress to the fall of the Third Reich in 1945, and the proclamation of the new State of Israel in 1948—has witnessed a Jewish national renaissance which can have no other explanation than that which the Hebrew prophets gave it centuries ago: "The Lord will set his hand again the second time to recover the remnant of his people" (Is 11:11).

The theme of this book traces the twentieth century fulfillment of the Hebrew prophets' ancient predictions concerning the return of the people of Israel back to their land. However, we have not only relied upon the Bible, which we believe to be the inspired Word of the living God, but we have also used liberally the *Haggadic* sections of the *Talmud*, along with the *Midrash* and the *Zohar*, plus the stories of the eighteenth century Hasidic rabbis. These works of sacred Jewish literature have been included in this book on Bible prophecy, not because we believe, as do Orthodox Jews, that the oral law, now transcribed in the Talmud, was given to Moses on Mount Sinai, and therefore determinent in formulating doctrine. The Talmud, whatever else it might be, is not a book of systematic theology. Theology is only casual and incidental in the Talmud. Its main concern is *Halakah*—the rule or norm for Jewish conduct.

The Talmud also contains *Haggadah*—stories, myths, legends, and the sayings of the sages, which are the homiletic interpretations of the law. Here we find the parables, the allegories, the tales, the nonauthoritative flights of fancy which so interestingly illustrate the Jewish way of life. In the

Talmud and the Midrash, the Messianic hope of Israel is most dramatically presented. It does not appear as a systematic doctrine, for the rabbis held different views about the Messiah. Some, like Hillel, even rejected the idea of a Messiah. However, the Messianic hope is so persistent in the Talmudic era because of the recent fall of Jerusalem in A.D. 70 and the subsequent terror which was spread by the Romans after the Bar Kokhba revolt. Some rabbis, like Rabbi Johanan Ben-Zakki, the reorganizer of the Sanhedrin at Jabne, were so certain of the near advent of the Messiah that he instructed his students at his death to have a throne ready, for the coming of the Son of David would not be delayed. Written in an era of great Messianic expectation, this sacred Jewish literature has many stories which will illuminate our understanding of what the Bible predicts about the coming of the Messiah and the regathering of the Jews back to the land.

The writing of this book afforded the author a unique experience. The entire manuscript was read in his presence by an Orthodox rabbi. Each page was read aloud, discussed and criticized, and in some cases corrected when an inaccuracy occurred. Obviously, the rabbi did not concur with the Messianic identity found in this book. However, his observations were invaluable. The author expresses his deep appreciation to Rabbi Bernard Schwab of the Ohavey Zion Synagogue in Lexington, Kentucky, who read the manuscript. In addition, the author expresses his gratitude for many hours of enlightening study in which Rabbi Schwab shared with him his learning in the Hebrew language and literature.

1

ISRAEL IN THE SECOND EXILE

IT WAS NEAR two o'clock on the afternoon of August 16, 1949, when an airplane, flown by an American pilot, appeared over the Mediterranean coast of Israel. Immediately it was joined by four fighter planes from the Israeli air force. That day this plane had flown from Austria. It carried the remains of a Jew who had died forty-five years before and whose body had slept quietly, all these years, wrapped in a blue and white flag of Zion, in a cemetery in Vienna. The grave in which it had been interred was an ordinary grave like many others there. A tall stone, surrounded by a wrought iron railing, over which ivy had crept through the passing years, made it indistinguishable, until one noted something else. Above, below, and on all sides of the stone and the railing, there was handwriting in Hebrew, Russian, and German. These writings were not desecrations. Rather, they were expressions of reverence felt by thousands of Jews who had visited that grave since 1904. The writings contained requests, hopes, prayers, proverbs, and blessings. Coming from all parts of the world, Jews had expressed in many different languages their longing for a national home in Israel and their appreciation to the man whose body lay there for his leadership in the ultimate fulfillment of this divinely implanted aspiration.

And now, in 1949, only one year after the new State of Israel had been formed, the body of that man was being brought to Israel, where it would lie in the sacred soil of Givat Herzl outside Jerusalem. As the plane landed at Lydda airport, it was surrounded by an honor guard of

11

Israeli soldiers, sailors, and air force men, holding aloft unsheathed sabers. The metal coffin, encased in a wooden box and covered with a prayer shawl, was lifted reverently from the plane and placed upon a black bier. Minutes later it lay in state upon a catafalque on the Mediterranean Promenade of Tel Aviv. Thousands of Jews quietly passed that coffin in solemn procession. At dawn a vast caravan of cars wound its way up through the hill country of Judea to place the coffin on a little ridge outside Jerusalem. In groups of ten, farmers, businessmen, workers, old settlers, and new immigrants walked by emptying the soil from three hundred Jewish settlements in the Holy Land into that grave to cover the coffin. A rabbi read the Kaddish, the prayer for the dead. Drums sounded. The great crowd, estimated at over one hundred thousand, sang "Hatikvah," the Zionist anthem. On that occasion, Prime Minister David Ben-Gurion said, "This is the second most important return of a dead hero to Israel in Jewish history. The first occurred over 3,300 years ago when the body of Joseph was returned in a coffin from Egypt."

Laid to rest in the soil of his beloved fatherland was the founder of modern political Zionism, Theodor Herzl. This man, whom David Ben-Gurion called "the seer of the Jewish State of Israel," was not the first Zionist, but he was the most successful one. He was "the first statesman the Jews have had since the destruction of Jerusalem," declared Israel Zangwill in 1901.

Mordecai said of Queen Esther, "who knoweth whether thou art not come to the kingdom for such a time as this?" (Est 4:14). In the providence of God, she was in a strategic position to help save her people, the Jews, from the destruction promised by Haman. Just so, in the providence of God, Theodor Herzl was raised up to bring Israel's longing for the land to fruition and fulfillment in the Zionist movement. Though he never saw Zionism's aspirations fulfilled in his lifetime, he initiated the movement that would lead Israel out of her wilderness wanderings in the second exile and back to the land.

The name *Zionism* was given to this movement of Jews back to the land in 1893 by Nathan Birnbaum. Originally,

Zion was King David's fortress which he purchased from the Jebusites. The prophets used the name *Zion* for the entire city of Jerusalem, but especially for the temple area. It also stood for the whole land of Israel. In the Middle Ages, the term *Zion* came to stand for the entire cultural heritage of the Jews—past, present, and future. However, since "Zion is where the Jew lives as a Jew," it must ultimately be a place and not just an ideal. Therefore, the term *Zionism* has become universally accepted to designate both the aspirations of the Jews to return and the actual process by which the return was made possible.

The Jews' immediate interment of Zionism's greatest leader on Mount Herzl soon after they had achieved sovereign statehood was a symbol of the fulfillment of their desire for a national home in the Holy Land. Centuries ago, in his commentary on the Torah, Rabbi Bahai had said, "The land is Israel's everlasting possession, which only they shall inherit and in which only they shall settle, and if perchance they are exiled from it they will return to it again, for, it is theirs in perpetuity and no other nations." This longing for *Eretz Israel*—the land of Israel—smoldered in the hearts of Jewish people for almost two thousand years during their second exile before it was to find fulfillment. "All the weaning of the centuries, all the enlightenment of modern times, have been unable to banish a longing for that land from their hearts," wrote David Kaughman in 1877, just as modern Zionism was about to dawn.

For generations the Jews had repeated the words of Ezekiel, "Thus saith the Lord GOD, I will gather you from the peoples, and assemble you out of the countries where ye have been scattered, and I will give you the land of Israel," (Eze 11:17). Orthodox Jews even arose at midnight to pray for the return. Even though in all their history the Jews had never occupied that little stretch of arid land on the eastern shores of the Mediterranean for more than a few centuries at a time, the land was theirs, for the covenant God of Israel had promised it to them (Gen 12:7). Their longing to return was never requited.

During the Middle Ages a Hebrew poet, Judah Halevi, who died in 1140, expressed it like this:

> In the East, in the East is my heart,
> And I dwell at the end of the West;
> How then shall I join in your fastings,
> How then shall I share in your jest?
>
> . . . .
>
> All the beauties and treasures of Spain
> Are worthless as dust, in mine eyes;
> But the dust of the Lord's ruined house
> As a treasure of beauty I prize!

This innate longing for a reunion between the land and the people was for all the centuries of the second exile dramatically reawakened each year at Passover time. On this night, which was different from all other nights, worldwide Jewry would remember the land of Israel. When the master of the house uncovered the matzo and lifted the plate for all to see, the recital of the Haggadah would begin: "This is the bread of affliction which our forefathers ate in the land of Egypt. All who are hungry—let them come and eat. All who are needy—let them come and celebrate the Passover with us. Now we are here; next year may we be in the land of Israel. Now we are slaves; next year may we be free men." Then with the conclusion of the seder, the great exclamation is made:

> Ended is the Passover Seder
>   According to custom, statue and law.
> As we were worthy to celebrate it this year,
>   So may we perform it in future years.
> O Pure One in heaven above,
>   Restore the congregation of Israel in Your love.
> Speedily lead Your redeemed people
>   To Zion in joy.
>   Next year in Jerusalem!

Wherever Jews lived outside the land, they never forgot it. Each year they would celebrate *Pesach* (Passover), *Shabuoth* (Pentecost), and *Sukkoth* (Feast of Tabernacles) according to the seasons in Palestine—spring, early harvest, and full harvest. When ice and snow covered the ground in northern Europe, the Jews would plant trees to celebrate *Tu-b' Shebat*, which was tree-planting time in Palestine. Amid downpours of rain in eastern Europe, Jews would pray for rain, for it was the dry season in the Holy Land. On *Tishah-b'Av*, the day that commemorates the fall of the first and second temples, the Jews would fast and mourn the loss of their land. The final service of *Yom Kippur* ended, as did the Passover seder, with "Next year in Jerusalem!" When a Jew prayed, he would face toward Jerusalem. During times of mourning, the bereaved family would be consoled with the words: "May God comfort you along with all the mourners of Zion and Jerusalem!" Every household kept a portion of earth from the Holy Land, and when a member of the family died, some of this dirt from Palestine was placed in the grave.

There is a Jewish legend which comes to us out of the Middle Ages which vividly expresses these Jewish aspirations for the land. A knight who went to the Holy Land to assist in the liberation of Jerusalem, left behind him a very dear friend. While the knight fought valiantly on the field of battle, his friend spent his time, as heretofore, in the study of the Talmud, for his friend was none other than a pious rabbi.

Months afterward, when the knight returned home, he appeared suddenly at midnight, in the study room of the rabbi, whom he found, as usual, absorbed in his Talmud. "God's greeting to you, dear friend," he said. "I have returned from the Holy Land and bring you from there a pledge of our friendship. What I gained by my sword, you are striving to obtain with your spirit. Our ways lead to the same goal." While thus speaking, the knight handed the rabbi a rose of Jericho.

The rabbi took the rose and moistened it with his tears, and immediately the withered rose began to bloom again in its full glory and splendor. And the rabbi said to the knight, "Do not wonder, my friend, that the withered rose bloomed again in my hands. The rose possesses the same characteristic as our people: it comes to life again at the touch of the warm breath of love, in spite of having been torn from its own soil and left to wither in foreign lands. So will Israel bloom again in youthful splendor; and the spark, at present smoldering under the ashes, will burst once more into bright flame."

Israel's second exile began when the Great Revolt against

Rome was put down in A.D. 70. By A.D. 135, when the second revolt under Bar Kokhba was suppressed by the Romans, the Jews' destiny was settled. For the next 1813 years the Jews would range over the earth to seek assimilation among the nations. But they were never to find relief from persecution and oppression which this loss of identity through assimilation would afford them. God's purpose for the nation Israel was not ended when she rejected Jesus as Messiah and thus exposed herself to the punishment and dispersement of the Roman holocaust in A.D. 70 and again in 135. Though Israel would be scattered, she would be kept. Though she would be hounded and persecuted, she would not completely disappear; for God is not finished with His covenant people, Israel.

The scattering of Israel came in A.D. 70 at the hands of the Romans. However, the reason for the scattering lay in the people of Israel themselves. Centuries before —even before the first exile in Babylon—during the reign of King Manasseh, God had reminded His people that scattering would be the unique consequence of their disobedience. "God said to David and to Solomon his son, In this house, and in Jerusalem, which I have chosen out of all the tribes of Israel, will I put my name for ever: neither will I any more remove the foot of Israel from off the land which I have appointed for your fathers, if only they will observe to do all that I have commanded them, even all the law and the statutes and the ordinances given by Moses" (2 Ch 33:7-8). Israel's refusal to obey God necessitated the first exile in Babylon. Their arch defection—the rejection of the Lord Jesus Christ as Messiah—brought about the second exile which began in A.D. 70.

It was for this reason that Jesus said, as He left the temple in Jerusalem, "O Jerusalem, Jerusalem, that killeth the prophets, and stoneth them that are sent unto her! how often would I have gathered thy children together, even as a hen gathereth her chickens under her wings, and ye would not! Behold, your house is left unto you desolate. For I say unto you, Ye shall not see me henceforth, till ye shall say, Blessed is he that cometh in the name of the Lord" (Mt 23:37-39). The Talmud says "Exile atones for everything."

Israel spent the next nineteen centuries in this atonement. However, even this cannot atone for her sin. At best, it only readies her to finally accept God's offer of atonement through the Lord Jesus Christ.

The idea of exile suggests compulsory banishment. The Diaspora can imply a voluntary absence from the land. The Jews were exiled for the first time in 587 B.C. when the Babylonians destroyed Jerusalem and the first temple. But when the seventy years were passed and the Jews were allowed to return to Judah, many chose to remain in Babylon rather than to come home. At that point they ceased to be exiles and became part of the Diaspora, for exile becomes Diaspora when the Jews who could return to their homeland choose not to do so. There are no exiles today—only the Diaspora, for any Jew who wishes to return may do so. It is for this reason that we date the second exile from the Great Revolt in A.D. 70. It lasted until the founding of the new State of Israel in 1948. During this period the Jews were in exile.

Now the second exile is over because the Jews have a homeland to which they can freely return if they wish. If they do not choose to do so, they remain a part of the Diaspora, but not exiles. There are two characteristics that mark the long centuries of the second exile, according to Hebrew University's Professor Ben Zion Dinur. One is the gradual disappearance of the specific Jewish character of Palestine and the emergence of a different national majority in that country. The other is the survival of the Jewish nation and the preservation of its national character outside its own land in this period when the land ceases to be Jewish.

The Great Revolt which marks the beginning of the second exile, ran its course between the years A.D. 66 and 70. The fall of Jerusalem occurred in A.D. 70. However, the fortresses of Herodium and Machaerus were yet to be taken. In addition there were almost a thousand Jewish Zealots who held out against the Romans at the mountain fortress of Masada, down near the Dead Sea. It took several more years for the Romans to subdue them. The Great Revolt itself lasted for nearly five years.

The Jews had never reconciled themselves to Roman occupation since its beginning in 63 B.C. Small uprisings had occurred in Galilee as early as A.D. 7 (cf. Ac 5:37). However, it was not the presence of the Romans in Judea which antagonized the Jews so much as it was a series of petty and corrupt Roman procurators who aggravated the situation. Overt rebellion against Rome started in A.D 66 when the Jews of Caesarea were mobbed by the Greek population of the city and the Roman authorities did not attempt to stop them—even though Caesarea was the capital of the province of Judea. The Jews in Jerusalem retaliated by wiping out the Roman garrison there. As a result of this provocation, the Twelfth Roman Legion marched against Jerusalem. However, it was unable to breach the walls. Later, retreating toward the sea, the Roman army was caught in the narrow pass of Beit Horon and was completely routed.

The "valley of Ajalon," entry to the mountains of Judah, is memorialized in Israel's first great epic poem (Jos 10: 12-13), for here it was that Joshua had commanded the sun to stand still. Judas Maccabee had fought and defeated the Seleucid army of Antiochus IV here in this valley. He was later killed here. This valley was strategic as the avenue of the Crusaders' advance upon Jerusalem in the eleventh century A.D., as well as in the defeat of the Turks by the Allied forces in 1917. Here in this valley which runs between Jerusalem and Jaffa on the coast, the Roman legion under the command of General Cestius Gallus, fled in unaccustomed confusion before the rebelling Jews—as the Amorites had fled before Joshua in the long ago. The Jews captured both ordinance and supplies which they hauled back to Jerusalem.

The Roman army was the largest the world had ever seen. It was composed of well over a half-million troops. There were thirty Roman legions, ten of which were in marching distance of Judea. A legion numbered about five thousand men plus auxiliaries composed of cavalry, archers, and light infantry. Their heavy artillery was capable of breaking down any wall, given enough time and the right deployment.

In A.D 70 the Jews had no army at all. They did not even have a military leader who could take command of the revolt. For the first few months, the priests attempted to direct the insurrection. Commanders like Josephus, who later defected to the Romans, were sent to take charge of the frontier

outposts in Galilee. The attempts of the priests to provide
leadership soon failed, as Judea inwardly collapsed into
anarchy. Zealots and priests contended with one another for
control. When in Jerusalem the Sanhedrin was annihilated
and many priests were killed, the Zealots turned upon each
other. Finally the city was divided between two Zealot leaders. Shimon Bar-Giora* commanded the western part of the
city, while Yohanan of Gush-Halav in Galilee commanded
the eastern side of the city, including the temple area. While
the best general the Romans had—Vespasian, the conqueror
of Britain—was moving south, destroying all in the path of
his three legions, the Zealots were fighting among themselves in Jerusalem. The defenses of the city were neglected
in the turmoil of civil conflict. Vespasian systematically cut
off potential aid from the Jews in Babylon and Egypt by
blocking the territory across which they could march. It took
four years for Jerusalem to be isolated by the Romans.

Following the death of Nero there was a struggle for the
throne of the empire. With the murder of Vitellius in late
December of A.D. 69, Vespasian was destined to reign.
When Vespasian returned to Rome, the conflict in Judea
was left to the command of Titus, his son, whom the Talmud
never mentions without appending the sobriquet, "the evil
one." Titus had four Roman legions under his command.
Besides the fifth, tenth, and fifteenth which his father had
brought, the twelfth was already stationed in Syria and had
been involved in the conflict from the very first. In the spring
of A.D. 70, Titus had surrounded Jerusalem and had set up
his camp at the present site of the King David Hotel. The
city was most vulnerable from the north—although three
separate walls must be breached from that direction in order
to reach the inner city. Only once in history was Jerusalem
taken from any direction other than the north. During the
Six-Day War in 1967, the city was taken through St.
Stephen's Gate on the western side of the Old City which
overlooks the Mount of Olives. Titus did not have para-
troopers to drop behind the wall and open the gates from the

---

*Many believe that David Green, a Polish-born Jew who came to live in
Palestine in 1906, took his new name from this Zealot leader. We know him as
Israel's first prime minister, David Ben-Gurion.

inside. He did have siege platforms which could tower above the walls, allowing his soldiers to shoot down upon the Jews inside. This platform, plus three battering rams, was moved to the north wall which was located then about 150 yards northwest of the Jaffa Gate, along the line of the present wall.

After days of constant battering, the wall fell and the Roman soldiers poured in. Five days more pounding, and the second wall fell. This time the Roman soldiers were pushed back, and the breach in the second wall was shored up. Another four days, and the second wall fell. The Jews retreated toward the temple mount. A month of bitter fighting followed before the Romans finally broke into the temple on the ninth of Av. Another month, and the Jewish resistance was ended in Jerusalem. Titus returned to Rome in triumph. Josephus says, "So neither its great antiquity, nor its vast riches, nor the spread of our nation all over the world, nor the greatness of the veneration paid to it on religious accounts, were sufficient to preserve it from being destroyed. Thus ended the siege of Jerusalem."[1] And thus began Israel's long exile.

As an aftermath of the fall of Jerusalem, Shimon Bar-Giora, who had commanded the defense of the western half of the city, was dragged through the streets of Rome and into the forum, where he was executed. Rome was also treated to a fabulous display of spoils and prisoners which Titus brought back from Judea. In the forum, the Arch of Titus was erected to commemorate the victory. On this beautiful arch, in bold relief, are carvings of the menorah and other vessels from the temple. Even today, Orthodox Jews avoid walking under the arch. But there is another monument in Rome which also commemorates the fall of Jerusalem. It is the greatest symbol of barbarism ever built by man—the Colosseum, which was constructed largely with Jewish slave labor brought to Rome after the Great Revolt.

Standing on the Portico of Octavia, the emperor Vespasian reviewed the triumphant return of Titus' army from the conquest of Judea. Thousands of slaves also filed by, as the emperor and his son gloated over their suppression of the Great Revolt. These slaves were destined to the games or to be used as forced labor in the construction of the Colosseum. *Judea divicta* (Judea conquered) and *Judea capta* (Judea captive) were inscribed on Roman coins which circulated the empire to remind all the people of the futility of revolt. The people got the message, for only one city ever revolted against Rome. That was Jerusalem. Tribes in Gaul and in other parts of the empire had revolted. But they could choose their battlefields, or even flee if they wished. But the Jews revolted, knowing that the Roman legions would soon appear before the walls of their city.[2]

The Roman emperor claimed the entire country as his own private possession. Only to eight hundred veterans did he give grants of land at Emmaus near Jerusalem. The rest of the land was divided up into lots and sold to the highest bidder. Thousands of Jews had been killed during the revolt; Titus massacred more in revenge. Others were made to fight in the arena; still others were sold into slavery. All who had taken up arms were either dead, enslaved, or banished. The infuriated conquerors spared neither women nor children. The second exile had begun amid terror and cruelty that was not even known when Nebuchadnezzar destroyed the city at the beginning of the first exile, six hundred years before.

In spite of the decimation which the Jews suffered, this was not the last revolt. Another Jewish revolt against Rome was to follow in a little over half a century, A.D. 132-35.

The roots of this second revolt were many. Sixty years had passed since the Great Revolt in A.D. 70. In Jewry a new generation had arisen. They had inherited the zeal of their fathers. They remembered the former independence of their people. Rebellion was again in the air. It had broken out among the Jews during the reign of Trajan, between A.D. 115 and 117, in Babylon, Egypt, Cyrenaica, Libya, and on the isle of Cyprus. On one occasion Trajan's wife wrote to him, "Instead of subduing the barbarians, you should rather punish the Jews who revolt against you." She sensed the rebellion of the Jews in a personal way, for, as tradition has it, she had given birth to a son on the Ninth of Av. That child died on the Feast of Dedication (Hanukkah). Since the Jews fasted on the Ninth of Av, she interpreted this as sorrow for the child's birth. And since the Jews rejoiced on the Feast of

Dedication in memory of the victory of the Hasmoneans, she interpreted this as a personal affront, believing that they were rejoicing at the emperor's sorrow. Revolution lurked for another decade or so. During that time there were many things that added up to the final outbreak in A.D. 132-35. Hadrian came to the throne in August of A.D. 117. To quiet the spirit of insurrection among the Jews, he promised to rebuild the temple. Later he gave up the idea because of the objections of the Samaritans. When the Jews heard of Hadrian's change of plans for rebuilding the temple, they were gathered together in the Valley of Beth-Rimmon, on the plain of Jezreel. An armed revolt was then and there threatened. In order to quiet the people, Rabbi Joshua told them the story of the lion and the stork. Having eaten his prey, a lion discovered that he had a bone stuck in his throat. In terror, he promised a great reward to anyone who could extract the bone. A long-necked stork accepted the challenge, performed the operation, and claimed the reward. Whereupon the lion refused to give him the reward, but instead gave him a mocking reply, "Rejoice that you have withdrawn your head unharmed from the lion's jaw!" "In like manner," said Rabbi Joshua, "let us be glad that we have escaped unscathed from the Romans."

Other reasons for the second revolt are given by various classical writers. Dio Cassius wrote in his *Roman History*, "At Jerusalem he [Hadrian] founded a city in place of the one which had been razed to the ground, naming it Aelia Capitolina, and on the site of the temple of the god he raised a new temple to Jupiter. This brought on a war of no slight importance nor of brief duration, for the Jews deemed it intolerable that foreign races should be settled in their city and foreign religious rites planted there."[3]

The Talmud has an interesting story about the revolt. It says, "It was the custom when a boy was born to plant a cedar tree and when a girl was born to plant a pine tree, and when they married, the tree was cut down and a canopy made of the branches. One day the daughter of the Emperor was passing when the shaft of her litter broke, so they lopped some branches off a cedar tree and brought it to her. The

Jews thereupon fell upon them and beat them. They reported to the Emperor that the Jews were rebelling, and he marched against them" (Gittin 57a).

Hadrian's biographer, Spartianus, writing in the third century, said that the second revolt was brought on by an edict of Hadrian which forbade circumcision. The emperor Domition had forbidden castration. Hadrian had extended the order to forbid all mutilation of the genitals, which of course included circumcision. This infuriated the Jews because they were hereby denied the ancient symbol of their covenant relationship with the God of Israel.

But whatever the causes, before long, Hadrian had a full-scale rebellion going in Judea. Tinnius Rufus, the Roman governor of Judea, was unable to cope with the massive uprising. It would appear that as a result of this rebellion, within a single year, the Romans had been forced to evacuate all of Judea, Samaria, and Galilee. It became apparent to Hadrian that he was up against a formidable foe, for the Jewish forces were led by a warlike messiah named Bar Kokhba.

The second revolt lacked a brilliant historian like Josephus, who had described the vivid events of the Great Revolt. Therefore, few details of the second revolt are known. Not the slightest trace of the ancestry of the leader Bar Kokhba can be found. He suddenly appeared as the incarnation of the people's will to revolt against Rome in order that they might recover their sovereign nation. In 1951, Bedouin antiquities hunters in the Dead Sea area found a cave containing some fragments of leather inscribed with Hebrew and Greek words. Among them was a document which contained the words, "From Shimeon ben Kosiba to Yeshua ben Galgoula and the people of the fort, Shalom." They belonged to the Bar Kokhba period. It is possible that these fragments give the real name of the great leader of the second revolt: "Shimeon Bar-Kosiba." Actually the name was written *KSBA*. However, the name was also written in Greek in some other letters which were later found. The Greek indicates that his name was pronounced *Kosiba*. For the first time the riddle of his name was solved. Those who believed that Bar Kokhba was the Messiah changed the *S* in his name to *KH*—hence, "Kokhba," or "the son of a star," in supposed fulfillment of Numbers 24:17. His enemies, and perhaps those disillusioned by the collapse of his movement, changed the *S* to *Z*, and thereby distorted the meaning of his name to read, "son of a liar."

As a result of the grief over the fall of the second temple in A.D. 70, Messianic expectation in the years that immediately followed took on a new impetus. It was natural that the people should look for the Messiah, who would take ven-geance upon the Romans who desecrated the sanctuary. The strong belief in a Messiah who would restore Israel to the land in all its pristine glory is the only way to explain the revolt under Bar Kokhba. Rabbi Akiba, who must have seen the fall of the second temple, became the spiritual leader of Bar Kokhba's ill-fated rebellion, and inspired the people to look upon Bar Kokhba as Messiah-King, though Bar Kokhba was not of the house of David and had done no miracles. He certainly was not noted for his great piety either, for Bar Kokhba had antagonized many of the rabbis when he exclaimed, "Lord, you need not help us but don't spoil it for us either!" The attempt to apply the "star" which should come out of Jacob (Num 24:17) to Bar Kokhba, indicates that he was regarded as Messiah. However, not everyone accepted Bar Kokhba as Messiah. The Jerusalem Talmud quotes Rabbi Simeon Ben-Yohai as saying, "Rabbi Akiba declared that Bar-Koziba is Messiah and should be called Bar-Kokhba. When Rabbi Akiba called Bar-Koziba, Messiah, Rabbi Johanan Ben-Torta exclaimed, 'Akiba, grass will grow in thy cheeks before the Son of David comes'" (Midrash R. Lam. 2.4).

How could such a great rabbi as Akiba Ben-Joseph be deceived? During the time of the Spanish persecution of the Jews, a Messianic speculator named Don Isaac Ben-Judah Abarbanel (1437-1509) wrote of Rabbi Akiba's belief in Bar Kokhba's messiahship, saying, "it happens to every wise man that he thinks and believes what his heart desires." The delusion of Rabbi Akiba can be explained in no other way. His longing for the redemption of Israel blurred his judgment about Bar Kokhba.

To contend with this mighty leader of the Jewish revolt,

Hadrian recalled General Julius Severus from Britain, where he was engaged in putting down a similar uprising. When he arrived in the east, General Severus found that the Jews were so firmly entrenched that he decided not to engage them in full force but to attack the Jews in small skirmishes. In preparing for this revolt against Rome, the Jews had determined not to repeat the mistakes of the Great Revolt. This time they had competent leadership. In the Great Revolt they had none. Furthermore, they prepared a number of fortified positions around the countryside, rather than risk being trapped in one fortress as their fathers had been sixty years before. Like General Vespasian, General Severus planned to prolong the war and to rely upon the scarcity of supplies to force the Jews into surrender. Some fifty small and separate engagements between Jews and Romans occurred, until the Romans finally had Bar Kokhba's stronghold of Bethar surrounded. Bethar was located on a hill a few miles southwest of Jerusalem. It overlooked a deep canyon. The position was a strong one, lacking only a sure water supply. Here the two greatest generals of the century stood face to face—General Julius Severus and Bar Kokhba. The siege of Bethar lasted for perhaps a year.

Bethar finally fell to the Romans in A.D. 135—the same day, according to the Talmud, on which the first and second temples fell—the ninth of Av (Tannith 26b). Several hundred thousand Jews were killed. The Romans also suffered great losses. In announcing the victory to the senate, Hadrian did not use the traditional formula for victory, "All is well with me and the army." Neither did the senate decree the emperor triumphant. Rather a medal was struck to commemorate the services rendered by the army. The coin bore the inscription *Exercitus Judaicus*, "Thanks to the army victorious over the Jews." What happened to Bar Kokhba is not known.

Judea was totally devastated and almost depopulated. Dio Cassius says that all Judea was well-nigh a desert.[4] Fifty fortresses and 985 villages were destroyed. Five hundred eighty thousand Jews fell in battle, while the number who died of wounds and starvation was never reckoned. The smell of death and decay was everywhere, for the Romans had forbidden the burial of the dead, in order that the sight and smell of corpses might serve as a warning to those who remained. "The corpses lay untouched," says the Talmud, "until Hadrian's successor, Antoninus Pius ordered their burial." All the towns which had offered resistance lay in ashes. For months after the fall of Bethar, Roman soldiers continued to hunt down and kill, or sell into slavery, fugitives and stragglers from the Jewish army, many of whom had hidden in caves. The slave market was so glutted that a Jewish slave was of less value than a horse.

Jerusalem was renamed *Aelia Capitolina*, after the emperor Hadrian himself. On the temple mount, the ground was plowed and leveled to erase any memory of the former sanctuary. There a temple of Jupiter Capitolinus was erected and a statue of the emperor Hadrian set up. Other Hellenistic buildings, such as theaters, a circus, public buildings, and pagan temples were erected. At the southern gate of the city, along the road to Bethlehem, the Romans placed the sculptured head of a pig. The Jews were banned under penalty of death from entering Jerusalem—Aelia Capitolina. Any who dared enter were crucified. The only time a Jew might enter thereafter was on the Ninth of Av, when, for a fee paid to the Romans, he could approach the temple area and mourn its destruction. Even the name of the land was officially changed from Judea to Palestine—the name of Israel's ancient enemies. In official records the "land of the Jews" became the "land of the Philistines."

The defeat of the Jews was not enough. Hadrian determined to break their spirit by forcing paganism upon them. The Jews experienced a religious persecution which they had not known since the days of Antiochus IV Epiphanes who, in the second century B.C., had attempted to impose Hellenism upon them by force. Since it was the Jews' religion which had held them together in spirit and had been one of the participating factors in the Bar Kokhba revolt, the Roman emperor seemed to think that the existence of the Jew could be terminated by banning his religion. No new rabbis could be ordained. On threat of death, observance of the Sabbath was forbidden. The ban upon circumcision, which had been one of the factors in the revolt, was continued. The reading of the Torah was denied. In the synagogues today a selection from the prophets is often read following the reading of the Torah. These passages from the prophets contain a reference to the Torah and are called *haftarah*. This practice originated, says the fourteenth century Spanish rabbi, David Abudarham, during the time of Antiochus IV Epiphanes, who had forbidden the reading of the Torah.[5] Therefore the Jews could hear, in the haftarah, a veiled reading of the Torah by way of the prophets. When Hadrian forbade the reading of the Torah, the reading of the haftarah served to keep the words of Moses before the people in spite of the emperor's edict.

Tinnius Rufus, the Roman governor who had been driven from the country during the first wave of the revolt, was returned and entrusted with the enforcing of the edicts of Hadrian. Rufus' treachery in searching out, by spies and informers, those who violated Hadrian's bans, was called by the Talmud "the time of severe persecution" or "the hour of danger."

In the days that followed the fall of Bethar, tens of thousands of Jews who had not met death during the revolt and who had escaped the aftermath of massacre, left Judea. The second exile was well underway. After the dispersement of A.D. 135 there was not another gathering of universal Jewry until the First Zionist Congress met in Bazel on August 29, 1897, and there would not be another sovereign state of Israel until the fourteenth of May, 1948. However, today, nearly two thousand years after the end of the Second Jewish Commonwealth, Jewish existence is still viable. The Roman Empire—Israel's conqueror—is lost in the dust of history, but Israel is alive today. In the Jerusalem Talmud, a learned rabbi said, "If a man asks thee: Where is thy God? Answer him: He is in the great city of Rome!" (Y Tannith 1.1). Meaning that the conquerors of Israel have in turn fallen, but Israel lives on.

Some of the desolation felt by the Jewish people in those days is reflected in the words of the fictional Rabbi Elisha who sums up the plight of the Jews: "The Temple gone, and the hope of rebuilding it, too. The land passing from under our control. Suffocating laws, crushing taxation. And our own ranks, especially in countries like Egypt, depleted by constant desertions to Christianity, Gnosticism, or unadulterated paganism. We have run our course."[6]

One night in 1960, a group of Israeli archaeologists met at the home of the president of Israel. Among them was not only the president, but also the prime minister, David Ben-Gurion, plus members of the Knesset, cabinet members, and other distinguished guests. Dr. Yigel Yadin, professor of archaeology in the Hebrew University of Jerusalem, presented a series of slides. On the screen there flashed an ancient Hebrew text written upon papyrus. Only recently this text had been discovered in a cave in the wilderness of Judea near the Dead Sea. Dr. Yadin read aloud from the colored photograph: "Shimeon Bar Kosiba, President over Israel." He then turned to the head of the modern State of Israel and said, "Your Excellency, I am honoured to be able to tell you that we have discovered fifteen dispatches written or dictated by the last President of ancient Israel 1800 years ago."[7]

It was during those eighteen hundred years that the people of Israel wandered upon the earth in the second exile, in fulfillment of the prophecy of Hosea: "For the children of Israel shall abide many days without king, and without prince, and without sacrifice, and without pillar, and without ephod or terpahim: afterward shall the children of Israel return, and seek the LORD their God, and David their king and shall come with fear unto the LORD and to his goodness in the latter days" (Ho 3:4-5). Though the entirety of this prediction of Hosea has not as yet been fulfilled in Israel, the regathering is being fulfilled even now. The stage is being set for the next great event—the second coming of Christ. Then Israel will seek the Lord, and David their king, as Hosea also predicted.

During the days of the Persian dominion of the Jews, Haman said unto king Ahasuerus, "There is a certain people scattered abroad and dispersed among the peoples in all the provinces of thy kingdom; and their laws are diverse from those of every people; neither keep they the king's laws: therefore it is not for the king's profit to suffer them. If it please the king, let it be written that they be destroyed" (Est 3:8-9). These words were spoken of Israel during the first exile.

However, things would not be much different during the long years of the second exile. Israel was *dispersed* for 1813 years. During this time, the Jew would maintain his *diversity*. However, it would be this very diversity that would cause a worldwide conspiracy against the Jew in which the nations would seek to *destroy* him. It is a simple fact of life that if one is sufficiently different, he will not be long tolerated. The Jew was different. This spelled potential destruction. If it had not been for the providential care of God—whose purpose for Israel is not yet completed—then this incompatibility would have meant the eradication of the Jew long ago.

The rabbis say in the Talmud, "One empire cometh and another perisheth away, but Israel abideth forever." Each year the Jews celebrate the Feast of Purim as a reminder of the time their forefathers were divinely protected from physical destruction during the first exile. Purim takes its name from a Persian word which means "lots," (cf. Est 9:24-26). During the Persian period of the first exile, wily Haman had cast lots to determine the appropriate day on which to exterminate the Jews. It fell on the thirteenth of Adar. However, as a result of the intercession of Ahasuerus' Jewish Queen Esther, the plans of Haman were frustrated, and the Jews were delivered. On the fourteenth day of Adar the Jews rested from the threat of extermination. On that date (in February or March) each year the Jews celebrate, with noisy jubilation, the Feast of Purim. During Purim the synagogue becomes a place of uproar—contrasted with the usual decorum which is there observed. It is customary to read the entire scroll of Esther during Purim services. When the name of Haman is read the congregation attempts to muffle the sound of his name by stamping, shouting, hissing, and laughing. The children also bring noisemakers to the service to help drown out the name of Haman.

The exile in Babylon demonstrated a unique quality in the people of Israel. This was their ability to maintain a national identity even though they had been removed from their homeland and had been dispersed among foreign peoples. Though other nations, when conquered, might maintain a viable identity as long as they remained in their home territory, only Israel has demonstrated this unique ability to retain her national identity in exile. This unique quality of the Jew was demonstrated during the first exile in Babylon. However, the ability of the Jew to flourish in exile has been a valid mark of Israel's uniqueness during all the years of the second exile also.

In his "Legend of the Just Men," Andre Schwarz-Bart tells the story of the ritual slap. Israel Levy was a shoemaker during the fourteenth century. When the Jews were expelled from England, Israel Levy wandered about, finally settling in France. He spent several years in the peaceful pursuit of his profession. There was a custom in Toulouse, where he lived, called the "Cophyz." On the eve of Easter each year, a representative of the Jewish community must fulfill this custom of long standing. He must appear, robed in a simple gown, before the cathedral, and there receive the ceremonial blow in the face administered by the Count of Toulouse.

Over the centuries the ceremony had been considerably refined, and the count contented himself with a symbolic slap administered at six paces. When the count died in 1348, his son followed him in the office held by his father. On the next Easter eve, he was to administer the ceremonial slap. Israel Levy appeared as the representative of the Jewish community to receive the indignity. He was barefoot, robed in a long shirt, and wore the prescribed pointed hat. Two yellow disks were sewn to his garment, front and back. Israel Levy was seventy-two years old when he received the ceremonial slap, which the son of the old count administered with great severity. The blow turned the head of the aged Jew, and his hat rolled to the ground. Picking his pointed hat off the ground, the old Jew thanked the young count three times, according to ancient custom. He then retraced his steps back through the jeering mob which had gathered to witness this amusing abuse of the Jews. When Israel Levy arrived at his home, he told his wife, "It is only a matter of habit, and I am already entirely accustomed to it." But, says the legend, "over the cheek, marked by four fingers, his left eye wept, and during the night that followed, his aged blood turned slowly to water. Three weeks later he displayed signal weakness by dying of shame."[8]

Through the centuries, Israel has been subjected to many such indignities. Yet, though many individual Jews have died of persecution and shame as Israel Levy died, the nation has not died of weakness and shame. She has persisted in spite of all the injustice, insults, and physical abuse with which the Gentile world has scorned her.

The earliest nonbiblical reference to Israel that we have is an inscription which was found on a pillar dating from the thirteenth century B.C. To celebrate his victories, Pharoah Merneptha of Egypt had written (c. 1220 B.C.) these words: "Israel is desolate, it has no seed left." But what of the Pharoahs who enslaved Israel and decreed their extinction? Where are they now? Mummified in museums and remembered with matzo balls! Some time later Mesha, king of Moab also wrote upon a victory monument: "Israel utterly perished forever!" But the very countries over which this ruler ruled—Moab, along with Ammon and Edom—are remembered today only because of their contact with Israel. Though many—from Pharoah Merneptha to Adolph Hitler—have tried to exterminate the Jew, he will not be exterminated. His presence today in the land, after nearly two thousand years of exile, is an unalterable testimony to the validity of the prophetic Word which declares that God's purpose for the nation was not terminated by Israel's rejection of Jesus as Messiah.

Two of the great modern theories of civilization are set forth in Oswald Spengler's, *The Decline of the West*; and in Arnold Toynbee's, *A Study of History*.[9] Spengler viewed history as a cycle in which civilization arose, flourished, and declined in inevitable doom. Therefore, each civilization has its own springtime of origin, its own summer of achievement, its autumn of decline, and its winter of death. Toynbee developed an evolutionary view of history in which he maintained that a nation could only survive if it made the necessary readjustments to each new crisis. If it made a right response to the challenges of history, it would continue in its cultural achievements. If it did not, it would perish. It is obvious that the history of the Jews did not fit into either of these schemes. Israel has persisted in a unique way in defiance of both Spengler's cyclic theory of the inevitable doom of all civilizations, and Toynbee's view of conditional doom. Israel is an historical anomaly, for she neither adjusted nor died! Nahum Goldmann says, "It [Israel] has survived because, despite all the so-called laws of history, its invincible will to do so produced ways of life that made possible its continued existence."[10] Max I. Dimont points out three fundamental differences between the Jews and other peoples that are indicative of their will to survive:

> First, there have been twenty to thirty civilizations in the history of mankind, the number depending on how one defines a civilization. The usual life span of a civilization as a culture-producing entity has been 500 to 1000 years. Then the civilization has either stagnated or disintegrated. The Jews are seemingly the only exception to this "rule." Second, the moment a people lost its country through war or some other calamity, that people either disappeared as an ethnic entity or regressed into meaningless existence. The Jews, however, though conquered time and again, though exiled from their homeland, did not die out. Against the odds of history, they survived for 2000 years without a country of their own. Third, no people except the Jews has ever managed to create a culture in exile. The Jews, however, in exile created not just one but six different cultures, one in each of the six major civilizations within which their history flowed.[11]

How do we account for Israel's survival? The Bible indicates that Israel has a manifest destiny. However, this manifest destiny is not so unassuming as the Reform Jews, for example, would have us believe. The Orthodox position is that exile is a result of sin. This is the teaching of Scripture and the position of many of the Talmudic rabbis. Ezekiel says, "The house of Israel went into captivity for their iniquity; because they trespassed against me." (Eze 39:23). Rabbi Jose Ben-Halafta in the Talmud says, "Woe to the children, for whose sins I destroyed My house, burnt My temple, and exiled My people among the nations! Woe to the father who had to banish his children, and woe to the children who had to be banished from their father's table!"

However, Reform Jewish philosophy rationalizes the exile and declares that it is the destiny of the Jews to teach universal brotherhood, tolerance, and good will to the nations among whom they have been scattered. Even if this be so, and one grant that the Jews have, in their exile, imparted a notion of tolerance and brotherhood to all the nations—this is not *the rationale* for Israel's dispersion and national survival which is presented in divine revelation. The Bible declares that God's purpose for Israel is not so much *pragmatic* as it is *eschatological*. God has an ultimate purpose for the nation Israel which has not yet been realized. Therefore, the final explanation of the persistence of Israel is this ultimate divine purpose, plus God's corresponding providential care for Israel, until such time as this purpose can be fulfilled in the course of history and prophecy.

However, there are many factors in the survival of the Jews during the second exile, between A.D. 135 and 1948, which indicate that the providence of God may be manifest in *pragmatic* terms within the *eschatological* framework. God does not just arbitrarily perpetuate the Jew. His preservation is a miracle. But this miracle of preservation has been manifest historically in the most practical and observable of ways during all the succeeding centuries of exile.

The first element in his two thousand year survival outside the land is the Jew's sense of historical identity.

A great seven-branched candlestand rises out of a small park before the Knesset, Israel's house of parliament in Jerusalem. On it is depicted scenes from Israel's history extending from the time of Abraham to the rebirth of the nation—a period of four thousand years. This menorah was the gift of the British parliament. When it was first erected, it caused a stir among Orthodox Jews who felt that the figures depicted constituted a violation of the second commandment. However, the late chief rabbi, Isaac Herzog, ruled that since only three sides of the figures protruded and the fourth was welded to another form, there was no transgression of the commandment. The twenty-nine scenes carved upon the menorah scan the course of Israel's history from the call of Abraham to the Warsaw Ghetto uprising, and from the wrestling of Jacob, whose name was changed to

Israel, to the proclamation of the new state in 1948. This is symbolic of the continuum of Israel's history. Whether in the land, or out of it, a real sense of historical unity and unique identity pervaded the people.

On one occasion, Sigmund Zimmel, a German Jew who was keenly interested in the "lovers of Zion" movement in Russia, came to Baron Rothschild in an attempt to enlist his financial aid for Jewish settlements in Galilee. These settlements, Yesud Hama'ala and Rosh Pinna had been founded by Polish and Romanian Jews. Rothschild, who had been the benefactor of many such colonies in Palestine, said, "Aren't you impressed by the remarkable fact that a Prussian Jew comes at the request of Russian Jews to a French Jew to enlist his aid for Romanian and Polish Jews living in Israel?" The national designations might differ. One may be German, Russian, French, Romanian, or Polish; but the fact that he is a Jew makes him one with all other Jews. Without this sense of history, the identity of the Jewish people would have been lost years ago.

During the long years of the second exile, this sense of historical identity was kept alive by several things. One was the intellectual life of the Jew which centered in the literature of the Torah and the Talmud. Both the Torah and the Talmud were a haven where the Jews of the Middle Ages could find refuge. This literature was not only a source of instruction and inspiration which engendered hope amid the anguish of the exile, but it was also a resource for unity. All Jews were one in the study of the Torah and the Talmud. Abba Eban, former foreign minister, says, "If the Bible was the Book Eternal, the Talmud was a daily companion. Prosaic, homely, practical, and replete with countless answers to human needs, to the men in the ghetto it was a reservoir of national life, the faithful mirror of an ancestral civilization in Babylonia and in Judea. In the face of outward hostility and of enforced segregation, the Jews of the Middle Ages were thrown inward on independent sources of memory and experience. Hostility helped to rally them around the traditions of their forefathers. They were aided in the cultivation of their separate identity by the regulations collected in Talmudic literature, which henceforth governed their life. The

Talmud offered an open door to a full, vivid, bustling world of Jewish experience, but an experience of human life by no means parochial."[12]

Throughout its history, Israel has been denied its sacred literature during many episodes of persecution. Antiochus IV forbade its use. Hadrian had it banned. Hitler had it burned. However, when a book could be secreted away and studied, it was. If not, what Torah and Talmud had been retained in memory by the rabbis was given verbally to devoted listeners, serving as an invisible source of unity and strength during times of severe repression and persecution.

Another unique feature which tended to keep the Jew separate was the dietary laws. Outside the land, the Jews were forced to maintain the dietary laws to guard against the danger of assimilation and to keep them distinctive as Jews. Rabbi Abba Bar-Zmina was a tailor, so an ancient story in the Jerusalem Talmud goes. Once, while working in the home of a Gentile, he was given meat to eat at dinner. Rabbi Abba refused to eat that which was not kosher. "Eat, or you will be killed," said the Gentile, The rabbi replied, "Do what you will with me, but I will not eat." The master of the house replied, "I will tell you the truth. If you *had* eaten, I would have felt like killing you. Since you are a Jew, be a Jew!"

Though the Old Testament forbade eating the flesh of the horse, rabbit, camel, along with many other unclean animals; it was the Jew's refusal to eat the meat of the hog that most distinguished him. During the Crusades and the Inquisition, suspected Jews were confronted with swine's flesh. Jews would expose themselves to torment and death rather than to touch this meat. Therefore, throughout history, when a people wanted to vilify the Jew, the symbol of that debasement was swine flesh, for they knew that enforced contact with a pig was most repugnant to the Jew. It is for this reason that some years ago the Knesset debated the restricting of swine raising in Israel. Not that all agreed that curbs on pig raising was necessary on religious grounds—for many in the Knesset were secularists and not religious Jews. But the issue was this: Abhorrence of swine has been a Jewish mark of identity for centuries. On grounds of heritage, the swine industry must be curbed in order to perpetuate this cultural mark of Jewish identity. And curbed it was by an act of the Jewish Parliament with the blessing of David Ben-Gurion, a nonobservant Jew, Israel's prime minister at the time.

Again, the sense of historical identity was kept alive during the Middle Ages and into the modern era by the religious environment in which the Jew existed while in exile. For centuries Jews have lived as a religious minority in predominantly Christian and Moslem countries. Yet the Jew continued to observe the laws of the Sabbath. Each Sabbath for two thousand years, Jews would gather together in synagogues for worship. This very act, apart from the significance of the worship service itself, served to distinguish the Jew from his Christian neighbors who met for worship on Sunday. The Midrash records that on one occasion the Roman emperor Hadrian was talking to Rabbi Joshua Ben-Hananiah. Said he, "I am better than your master Moses, because a live dog is better than a dead lion." Whereupon Rabbi Joshua replied, "I can prove to you that Moses is an exception to this text [Ec 9:4]. Issue a decree that no fires be lighted in all of Rome on the morrow." And so the decree was issued that in no Roman home should a fire be lit on the next day. Climbing to the roof of the palace, the Caesar and Rabbi Joshua stood looking out over the city. In a few minutes a wisp of smoke arose from a house. When Caesar's men had investigated, he was informed that a patrician was sick and the doctor had prescribed warm water for him. The Rabbi said to Hadrian, "You forbade a fire and yet on the slightest pretext your command was set aside. Moses forbade a fire fifty-two times a year on the Sabbath, and for many centuries his command prevails." Sabbath observance has perpetuated Jewish identity and has made them a separate people, as Ahad HaAm observes, "More than Israel kept the Sabbath, the Sabbath has kept Israel." A 1602 prayer book expresses it like this, "If a man keeps the Sabbath properly, the Lord also keeps him." For centuries, even when the Christian day of rest was forced upon the Jew, it was the uniqueness of the Sabbath which maintained for him the consciousness of his own identity. Even if his body could not rest on the Sabbath, his spirit observed it,

when, from sundown on Friday to sundown on Saturday, his
soul was in ancient Israel.

Rabbi Eleazar said, "Thou hast given us in love this great
and holy day." The rabbis have also said the Sabbath will
never be abolished in Israel. However, just that very thing is
happening in Israel today. The Sabbath is no longer observed, and many synagogues are empty, while the beaches
are full. Traditional forms of Jewish consciousness—such as
Sabbath observance and synagogue attendance—are being
lost, for they are no longer needed as an aid to maintaining
Jewish identity. Only during the high holy days are
synagogues in Israel crowded. The synagogue services and
ritual which have kept Jews together during the centuries of
the second exile are now neglected by older immigrants
coming to Israel, and are utterly rejected by many of their
children who were not raised in this tradition. Therefore, in
modern times we are seeing the unbroken tradition of the
Jews beginning to erode away. This erosion has been rapid
among the Reform Jews; slower among Orthodox Jews.
Conservative Jews have made a last-ditch attempt to synthe-
size the best of the old tradition with the way of life maintained by emancipated Jewry and thereby to retain the old
values in a modern world. But, surprisingly enough, it is in
Israel itself that these unique values, which attest to the
Jewish self-identity, are being lost in neglect.

For most of the second exile, Jewishness was retained by
still another factor in the viable identity of the Jew. This was
the ghetto which had existed since the tenth century A.D.
The Midrash says, "Why is Israel likened to an olive? Because as an olive's oil cannot be mingled with other sub-
stances, so Israel cannot be mixed with other peoples." The
ghetto helped to facilitate this separation. In 1516 the Vene-
tian Republic ordered all Jews segregated into an area called
Ghetto Nuovo. This act was to give the name to a uniquely
Jewish humiliation which was endured in Europe for
centuries—the isolation of the ghetto. Though the Jewish
people were always objects of hostility and persecution, and
though they were often ordered out of a country, from the
tenth century forward they were to experience this new
disgrace. They were to be herded together in political, so-

cial, and cultural isolation in this communal prison, the ghetto.

The ghettos of medieval Europe were intended to keep the Jews confined in a restricted area. They often had walls around them, and many had massive gates which could be bolted. This not only kept the Jews in, but also kept enemies out. Therefore, the ghetto was not only a place of confinement, it was also a place of security and protection—especially at Easter time when persecution from the Christian population was most likely to erupt. Ghetto life was regulated by Talmudic law. The ancient rabbis had said, "Build a fence about the Torah." This is what actually happened in medieval Jewry, for the Talmudic community operated within the walls of the ghetto as a defense against the church. Though the Talmud was at the hub of Jewish life to regulate communal living, the synagogue and the Torah schools in the ghetto were also important factors in preserving and keeping distinct the Jewish way of life. In an address to the First Zionist Congress, Max Nordau put it this way: "It is plain historical truth to state that only the ghetto gave the Jews a chance of surviving the terrible persecutions of the Middle Ages. In the ghetto the Jew had his own world; it was his sure refuge and it provided the spiritual and moral equivalent of a motherland. . . . In the ghetto all specifically Jewish qualities were esteemed. . . . In the moral sense, the Jews of the ghetto lived a full life."[13]

In addition, the ghetto had its own government and even developed its own language—Yiddish. Yiddish was developed out of the German vernacular in the thirteenth century, which the Jews generously laced with Hebrew words. This language was carried into the ghettos of Poland, Hungary, Russia, and Bohemia when the migration of Jews began to flow from the West back to the East as a result of persecutions in western Europe. Isaac Peretz, the Yiddish novelist, said of this language, it "will bear witness to the violence and murder inflicted upon us, bear the marks of our expulsion, from land to land, the language which absorbed the wails of the fathers, the laments of the generations, the poison and bitterness of history, the language whose precious jewels are the undried, uncongealed Jewish tears."[14]

The ghettos developed their own educational system also. This unalterable need for schools to perpetuate the Jewish heritage emerged even within the shadow of the Nazi terror in the new ghettos of World War II. After the creation of the Vilna Ghetto, in September, 1941, a group of teachers organized an educational system. The guiding principles of this ghetto educational system were the cultivation of love and respect for Jewish history and heritage. Special emphasis was placed upon the great movements for national independence in Jewish history, such as those of the Maccabees and Bar Kokhba. The recognition of the unity of the Jewish people, their universal struggle against injustice, their determination to rejuvenate the nation and their identity with the land, were stressed.[15]

The ghetto in Europe lasted for a thousand years. The Progue Ghetto dates from about A.D. 900. Since ghettos could not expand outward to encompass more territory, they pushed upward. Houses rose floor upon floor, until the ghetto era ended in the flames of World War II. All the while the ghetto was both protecting and restricting the Jew physically, it was also protecting and perpetuating a way of life that might have been lost had the ghetto not existed.

Another element in the Jew's historical identity is the Hebrew language. "Hebrew is the historical chain which links all the dispersed parts of our people into one national body," wrote Zacharias Frankel, the German Talmudist.[16] "It is the only glue that holds together our scattered bones. It also holds together the rings of the chain of time," says Peretz. "It binds us to those who built pyramids, to those who shed their blood on the ramparts of Jerusalem, to those who, at the burning stakes, cried, *'Shema Yisrael!'*"[17]

The Jews call the Hebrew language *lashon kedesh*—the sacred tongue. Jewish legend says that God will descend to earth only ten times between creation and the day of final judgment. One of these occasions was when He descended, along with seventy angels, to the tower of Babel. There the speech of man was confounded. God and the angels cast lots on that occasion. Each angel received a nation, but God received Israel. To each nation a particular language was assigned, but to Israel God Himself gave the very language that He used to create the world—Hebrew! Hebrew was used in Israel until the Babylonian exile. Then Aramaic became the spoken language of the era, spoken by Assyrians, Babylonians, and Persians. Though it died out in other regions, Aramaic continued to flourish in Israel after the exile. It was the language that Jesus spoke. Jews continued to use it until the fall of the second temple. Aramaic persisted as the language of the Talmud, while Hebrew all but died as a spoken language after the dispersement of the Jews. During the Middle Ages, Hebrew was kept alive in the synagogues. Nevertheless it served as a subtle force, for in worship it made all Jews one in spite of the diversified language which might be spoken through change of nationality.

The revival of Hebrew as a modern language—the only ancient language to be revived and used in the modern world—actually started before the beginning of the Zionist movement in the nineteenth century. It was begun on shipboard between Marseilles and Jaffa by a consumptive medical student named Elieser Ben-Yehuda. The year was 1880.

What Jews there were in Palestine at this time spoke either Yiddish or Arabic. Since Hebrew was rich in words which convey spiritual ideas, but was limited in what it could express in practical secular matters, Ben-Yehuda set about to ferret out long-forgotten words from ancient sources, and even to coin new words for a new Hebrew dictionary. Ben-Yehuda's infant son was the first child since the first century to be raised with Hebrew as his native tongue. His father even wrote some lullabies in Hebrew and taught his Russian-born wife to sing them. The child's only playmate seems to have been a snake which had crawled through the wall, since the boy had been isolated from other children who might introduce him to foreign words. The first word that the child uttered was the Hebrew word for snake. Ben-Yehuda fathered eleven children, each of whom grew up dedicated to the task of disseminating Hebrew.

Some of the Orthodox rabbis were horrified at the idea of using Hebrew, *halashon hakadosh*, for secular purposes. How could one tell a child to wipe his nose, or go to the bathroom, in the holy language! Theodor Herzl himself rejected the idea that ancient Hebrew could be revived and used in the new State of Israel. He assumed that German would be the national language, deriding the idea that a railway ticket could be purchased in Hebrew or that a child could be taught arithmetic in Hebrew. However, as the twentieth century got underway, Hebrew became established as the national language of the Jews living in Palestine. Though each new generation of immigrants from Europe posed a threat to the purity of the language, filling the gaps in their Hebrew vocabulary with foreign terms, Hebrew was recognized as the official language of Palestine when the League of Nations gave a mandate to the British to govern it. That was in 1922. For the first time since Bar Kokhba's revolt, Hebrew would appear on local coins.

By the time the new State of Israel was chartered by the United Nations in 1948, Hebrew was never again challenged as the national language, even though many ultra-Orthodox Jews felt that Hebrew should be reserved as the language of prayer and of the synagogue, as it was during the Middle Ages when it served as a subtle unifying force of all Jewry.

The Jew has an innate sense of common source. There is an identity between Jew and Jew that is common to all mankind and which is born out of the context of history, ancient, medieval, and modern. But there is another identity that is unique to the Jew. It is his common source—the land. One Jew's relation to another Jew is not unique. But his identity with the land is unique among mankind and is indigenous only to the Jew. Rabbi Zalman said, "The love for Zion must be as a fire burning in the heart of the Jew. He who wishes to be a true Jew must go to Palestine." Here is an immigrant from the ghettos of Europe who sets foot on the soil of Israel for the first time in his life. He is sure that he has come home! How is this conviction possible? It cannot be explained apart from this innate identity with *Eretz Israel*—the land of Israel. Perhaps this is more significant than actually possessing the land itself. For even when Jews were scattered among the nations and others possessed the Holy Land, it was still theirs in thought, if not in reality. This is why the Jews speak of going to the Holy Land as *aliyah*—"going up"—and *yishuv*—"settling down." The people were not returning to a strange land. They did not merely immigrate, but they were returning to their origins. From literature, from myth and legend and tradition but mostly from the ancient Scriptures, the Jews who returned knew the land well, even though they had never seen it before. They recognized the names of rivers, mountains, valleys, plains, towns, and villages. The map of Palestine was animated, for they also knew the historical events which had happened in the various localities. Their forefathers had actually stood, and had done great deeds, where they stood.

However, this longing for the land was not only something that was conditioned by such things as tradition, history, literature, culture, and the like. It was innate. Aliyah had an inner strength. It was something that was woven by the Lord himself into the very heart of the Jew. Therefore, the land is as much a part of Jewishness as is the Torah, the Talmud, the synagogue, the Hebrew language, circumcision, and the keeping of the Sabbath.

The Assyrian king Sennacherib failed to understand this unique and innate attachment which the Jew has for the land. When the Assyrians stood before the gates of Jerusalem in 701 B.C., a spokesman for the King of Assyria, Rabshakeh, said, "Make your peace with me, and come out to me; and eat ye every one of his vine, and every one of his fig-tree, and drink ye every one the waters of his cistern; until I come and take you away to a land like your own land, a land of grain and new wine, a land of bread and vineyards" (Is 36:16-17). But there was no land like their land, and the people of Judah refused to accept Sennacherib's offer. In 1903 Great Britain offered the Jews several thousand acres in their East African Protectorate of Uganda. The Jews could settle and find a new homeland there. Though this offer seriously jeopardized the Zionist efforts just before the death of Herzl, it was finally rejected—and for the same reasons their forefathers had rejected the offer of the Assyrians twenty-six centuries before. Israel has an attachment for the land which is woven into her very soul.

Over and over again the Talmud and other ancient Jewish literature expresses this sentiment. In commenting upon the unique significance of the land, the rabbis have made such statements as: He who resides in Palestine is without sins! He who resides in Palestine, reads the *Sh'ma*, and speaks Hebrew is a son of the world to come. Even the merest talk of the residents of Palestine is Torah. He who walks four ells (between nine and fifteen feet) in Palestine is assured of the world to come. Happy are they who dwell in Palestine, for they have no sin and no transgressions either in life or in death. Stones in the land of Israel are heavier than in other lands. Living in Israel is itself an atonement for sins. Nothing can be perfect, except in Israel. Residence in Israel is equivalent to the observance of all the biblical precepts. Prayers are more acceptable when uttered in Palestine. More beloved is a small school in *Eretz Yisrael* than a large academy outside of it. Living in *Eretz Yisrael* is equal to the weight of all *mitzvah.** All holiness comes by way of Palestine. One who goes to Palestine to attain holiness will achieve his aspirations. Even a Canaanite bondwoman, if she lives in *Eretz Yisrael*, is assured of belonging to the world to come. Sinning in *Eretz Yisrael* is worse than elsewhere—it is like rebellion right within the king's own palace. Each land has some unique property, but the land of Israel is endowed with all these, lacking none. Residents in Israel are in a holy atmosphere. Rabbi Nachman said, "While I am breathing and alive, I must go to Palestine. The absolute spirit and wisdom are found only in Palestine."

The Talmud indicates that one can think better in the land than he can outside of it. "When Rabbi Zeira came to Palestine he understood more clearly the arguments of his opponent Rabbi Illa, and surrendered his own viewpoint in a certain matter, saying, 'This demonstrates that the very air of Palestine makes one's brain clearer.'" "A student in Palestine grasps the reasons of a law twice as quickly as a student in Babylon. Even a Babylonian student who goes to Palestine becomes twice as keen as he who remains in Babylon." The Talmud even observes that a man may drown in all the waters of the world—but not in the Dead Sea!

Therefore the land sustains an unprecedented place in the

---

*A *mitzvah* is any biblical or rabbinic commandment, or any act of charity done in fulfillment of the law.

idea of Jewish self-identity. Though Reform Jews tend to downgrade this thesis, to the Orthodox, whose image is still uniquely Jewish, the land is inseparable from his understanding of himself and of his place in history. His existence may have meaning outside the land, but it will be made totally meaningful only within the geographic confines of the Holy Land whose borders were circumscribed by the covenant God of the patriarchs, Abraham, Isaac, and Jacob.

Besides Israel's sense of historical identity and her sense of identity with the land, Israel also has a sense of destiny. This sense of destiny is bound up in the Messianic hope of a golden age. Judaism has given to the world four great gifts: ethical monotheism, refined morality, the prophets of truth and righteousness, and a belief in the Messiah. The last one of these concepts is due to Israel's unique orientation. All other ancient peoples looked backward to a golden age in their past. This is the chief difference between Judaism and Hellenism. The Greeks and Romans saw the golden age at the beginning of their history. Only the Jews saw the golden age at the end of their history, and yet in the future as well. Since Israel has known only suffering and tribulation, it has known no glorious past. Therefore, the Jews always looked forward to a glorious future. This is expressed in a very subtle way by the famous quip of Rabbi Posner. Rabbi Zalman Posner was one of the few Jews to achieve wealth in nineteenth-century eastern Europe. When he drove his carriage through the streets of Warsaw, he was often stoned by an anti-Semitic mob. One day his servant remarked sadly, "Truly we are in exile, when worthless urchins throw stones at an important person like yourself." Rabbi Posner replied, "Don't worry about it. When the Messiah comes and we have our own State, they will drive in luxurious carriages, but *we* will throw stones!"

"Israel alone," says Abba Eban, "looked forward to a golden age in the future and interpreted history as a meaningful and progressive movement toward Messianic consummation. Thus Jewish thought marked a revolt against previous religions. Never before had a people conceived a vision of human destiny as something sharply different from the natural cycle, with its inexorable succession of birth, life,

and decay."[18] Though Reform Judaism has largely abandoned this hope of a personal Messiah who will usher in the
golden age, Orthodox Jewry still retains the hope. In fact,
this hope is so strong among some groups of ultra-Orthodox
Jews that they reject the present State of Israel because it is
secular and was not founded by the Messiah. These are the
naturei karta (guardians of the City.) These ultra-pietistic
Hasidim maintain constant opposition to the new State of
Israel from within, for most of them live in Israel, believing
that the land can only be legitimately recovered by the
Messiah.

Thus the past, present, and future tended to unify and
preserve the Jew as a unique and enduring people among the
ebb and flow of many other civilizations. Out of the past, he
had a sense of common origin—the land. In the present there
is the common identity forged by his religion, language, and
contemporary plight, which unified him. But as the Jew
looks toward the future, there is optimism for his is the hope
of a golden age to be ushered in by the Messiah. Maimonides
said, "I believe with perfect faith in the coming Messiah;
and, though he tarry, I will wait daily for his coming." It is
this belief in the coming Messiah that has sustained the Jew
during all the years of his exile and adversity.

The second exile ended on the fifth day of the Jewish
month Iyar in the year 5708—May 14, 1948—when
twentieth-century Israel became the first nation created by
the United Nations. The main impetus for the return of the
Jew to the Holy Land was political Zionism which began in
the last half of the nineteenth century. David Ben-Gurion
said, "The Eastern Jews continued to pray three times a day,
asking for their return to the promised land, but they left to
God, to Adonai, the job of arranging the operation. They did
not think to bring it about themselves. The Western Jews,
thanks to the realistic influences to which they were subjected, began to think in a different way: for heaven to help
you, you must help yourself."[19] Today the effort of the
Jewish people to recreate a home for themselves in Palestine
sounds quite sensible. But a century ago, when Zionism
began, not to wait for God's miracle of Messianic restoration was a revolutionary idea.

For the first fifteen hundred years of the second exile, Jewish movement had been toward the West. But, with the expulsion of the Jews from Spain in 1492 and the great persecutions which followed in Spain and Portugal at the beginning of the sixteenth century, Jewish migration turned backward toward their origins. Over three hundred thousand Jews who were unwanted in the West turned about to populate eastern Europe and the Middle East. By the middle of the nineteenth century, about seventy-two percent of world Jewry was living in eastern Europe.

On many occasions the plight of the Jew has been suggested as a way by which the integrity of any given nation can be measured. The Russian writer, Alexandra Kalmykowa said, "The social position of the Jews is the barometer indicating the moral condition of the nations."[20] Napoleon, while emperor of France, observed, "The treatment of the Jews in every country is the thermometer of that country's civilization." But not only does the treatment of the Jew indicate the degree of any given civilization, there was also a vital relationship between the state of European Jewry and the migration of Jews back to Palestine itself. During times of stability when the Jews were relatively free from persecution, migration was nil. But each new crisis in Europe set into motion a new wave of immigrants to Palestine. It happened when the Jews were expelled from Spain. It happened as a result of the persecutions which followed the bubonic plague. It happened as a result of the Russian pogroms in the 1880s. It occurred in association with the Hitler persecutions in the 1930s and 1940s. However, before the Zionist movement, Jewish return to Palestine was never anything but a trickle.

Palestine was a part of the Ottoman Empire when it fell to the British in World War I. The Turks had ruled the Holy Land for exactly four hundred years, 1517-1917. The land was stagnated by neglect, famine, earthquake, local wars, and the loss of trade routes due to the opening of a new way to India around the Cape of Good Hope. Though many learned rabbis and scholars, along with some tradesmen and artisans, had returned to the land during earlier centuries, the country lay largely deserted and deprived. The Turks were indifferent to its development, and the inhabitants were smitten with apathy.

The first modern colonizers of the land were Russian Jews (fifteen men and one woman) who came in 1882. They took the name *Bilu*—a Hebrew acronym which is taken from the initial Hebrew letters found in the words of Isaiah 2:5, "House of Jacob, come let us go." In fifteen years eighteen colonies were established and became a prototype of returning Israel. Therefore when the First Zionist Congress met in 1897, this early movement had already settled a number of Jews in the land. These were mostly university students, young men and women who had renounced their careers to go to Palestine and make a new life.

In May of 1881, Czar Alexander II of Russia was killed by a bomb. His son inherited the throne. Alexander II had been killed by a revolutionary plot in which a Jewess had been implicated. This was enough to place the blame upon the Jews. This gave rise to officially sanctioned mob riots in which a wave of massacres swept the Jewish population. Scores of Jews were murdered to the ringing of church bells. Thousands of other Jews fled Russia. Many others were expelled in the most brutal fashion. Those who remained found life intolerable. The May Laws passed during this time reduced many Jews to poverty because they denied the Jew a means of livelihood by refusing him access to the land, to the schools, or to the professions. With whatever efficiency the czarist government could exercise, it was determined to eliminate the Jewish population of Russia, whom it charged with the responsibility of all the existing evils from which the nation suffered.

The first widely published reaction to the Russian pogroms—a Russian word which means "devastation" or "destruction," and which is used of an organized massacre, especially of Jews—came from Leo Pinsker in 1882. He wrote a pamphlet entitled *Auto-Emancipation*, in which he advocated national liberation to a people who could be neither assimilated into their present society nor returned to the ghetto. Pinsker was a Jewish doctor from Odessa who believed that anti-Semitism was a psychosis which was inevitable in the human race. It was caused, he maintained, by the exile of the Jew among the nations and could only be cured when the Jew was liberated from his abnormal existence by being allowed to return to a new territorial base. This new emancipation of which Pinsker wrote and which he equated with a new territorial base, was the return of the Jew to his homeland in Palestine.

Theodor Herzl, the founder of modern political Zionism, did not know of Pinsker's writings, but he too was greatly distressed by the suffering of the Russian Jew. Herzl was born in Budapest in 1860. He was reared in a wealthy and cultured Jewish home. He was educated at the University of Vienna, from which he received a doctorate in law. However, he did not pursue a legal career, but became a columnist for the leading newspaper of Vienna, the *Neue Freie Presse*. He was the foreign correspondent for this paper in Paris between 1891 and 1896. It was during this time that the famous Dreyfus affair occurred. This was to become one of the most formidable factors in Herzl's Zionism.

Alfred Dreyfus was a French army officer who was accused of high treason and was court-martialed on the charge of passing military information to the Germans. Though the court had but meager evidence against him, Dreyfus was found guilty and condemned to degradation and to deportation for life. Herzl's experience in Paris during the Dreyfus case changed his whole outlook on life. Dreyfus happened to be a Jew. His trial released a virulent anti-Semitism in France, for the cosmopolitan ideals which brought about the French Revolution and subsequently, acceptance for the Jews, had by now, a century later, been replaced by a new nationalism. The Jew, in the late nineteenth century, had become a threat to national solidarity. Herzl declared that his Zionism began, not with the trial of Dreyfus itself, for he believed him to be guilty, but with the aftermath of the trial. Dreyfus was sentenced to Devil's Island. It was the brutality of the ceremony in which Captain Dreyfus was stripped of his rank that impressed Herzl. He believed that Dreyfus received a just sentence, but he could not comprehend why the spectators of Dreyfus' humiliation were so delighted. In an impressive ceremony an officer broke the traitor's sword. One by one a sergeant, a corporal, and a private stripped

Captain Dreyfus of his insignia and cast them at this feet. "Why are the people so delighted?" Herzl asked over and over again, as he witnessed the glee with which the people executed the humiliation of Dreyfus. "How can they find such intense joy in the suffering of a human being," he asked. A colleague replied to Herzl's question, "No, the French do not feel that he is a man. They see him not as a human being, but as a Jew. Christian compassion ends before it reaches the Jew. It is unjust—but we cannot change it. It has always been so, and it will be so forever!"

Herzl was not inspired by some vague utopian dream. Rather it was the misery of the Jew which he saw as the compelling force of political Zionism. This misery was being intensified every day by an emerging virile anti-Semitism which occurred in the late nineteenth century. Since the end of the French Revolution in 1789, the Jews had been experiencing a new freedom that spread to most of the other European countries. But suddenly, barely a hundred years later, a vicious anti-Semitism had broken out again. For centuries Christians had had ill regard for Jews because many felt that they were to be blamed for the death of Jesus. In addition, the Jew stubbornly refused to yield to Jesus as Messiah and Saviour. But now a new dimension was added to this old ambivalence. Jews came to be regarded as members of an inferior Semitic race which was a potential threat to a superior European civilization. Thus the incentive to hate the Jew took on a new element. Hitler used this notion of the superior versus the inferior race as the basis of his pogroms against the Jew. With the new element in anti-Semitism, the "conversion" of the Jew to Christianity would not solve the problem. The issue was more basic—in their blood—and therefore nothing short of enslavement and extermination would do. What was the Jew to do? He had no government to which he could turn for protection. Zionism had the answer. It was held by some that the only remedy for such anti-Semitism was auto-emancipation—the creation of a Jewish state.

Max Dimont points out the nature of this nineteenth century anti-Semitism. Its characterization is fourfold. First, there is prejudice, followed by an attempt on the part of the prejudiced to justify this bigotry. Second, anti-Semitism is directed toward the Jewish race, not toward individual Jews. Third, irrespective of how many others may be guilty of the same fault, it is the Jew who is the target of anti-Semitic hostility. Fourth, anti-Semitism is not in any way redemptive. It holds out no solution and offers no alternative to the Jewish plight.[21] Theodor Herzl realized that there was no viable solution to the problem apart from the Jewish state. Of the two concepts of Jewish existence extant in Herzl's day, neither would solve the problem of Jewish misery. One was the *ghetto concept*, which saw the absolute separation between Jews and other peoples and which held that until the Messiah comes to restore all things, the Jews must wait, helpless and dependent upon others. The other, the *assimilation concept*, was based upon the thesis that the Jews were not in any sense an independent nation like others. Rather, there was only a thin barrier of religion and custom that separated them from other citizens of the same country. If this could be liquidated, the Jew would soon lose his uniqueness through assimilation among his neighbors. Herzl had rejected the ghetto concept. As a result of the Russian pogroms, the Dreyfus trial, and the newly emerging anti-Semitism which was destined to sweep Europe, he was forced to give up the assimilation concept. The third alternative was *political Zionism*, which he set forth in his pamphlet, *The Jewish State*. In this book he gave the Jews a political purpose and the means to fulfill it.

Before the Zionist aliyahs began, there were less than fifty thousand Jews living in Palestine. They were centered largely in four cities, called "the four lands"—Jerusalem, Hebron, Tiberias, and Safad. They had no economic roots, for they were largely unproductive, living on monetary donations from abroad. They were more closely related to their origins in Europe than to each other, for they spoke different languages and maintained past ties, and each community lived largely independent of the other. The only thing they had in common was the belief that the Messiah would one day come and redeem their ancestral homeland. To world Jewry this little group of Jews were the vanguard who maintained a foothold in the Holy

Land pending the coming of the Messiah.

This was the situation in Palestine when Herzl wrote *The Jewish State*.

When Theodor Herzl returned to Vienna after the conclusion of the First Zionist Congress, he made the most famous prediction about the future of the nation Israel that is to be found anywhere outside the pages of the Hebrew prophets. In his diary he wrote: "If I were to sum up the Congress in one word, it would be this: at Basel I founded the Jewish State. If I were to say this today, I would be greeted with universal laughter. In five years, perhaps, and certainly fifty, everyone will see it." The entry is dated August 29, 1897. Fifty years and nine months later, Herzl's prophecy came true. With the declaration by the United Nations and the historic transaction in the Tel Aviv Art Museum on May 14, 1948, the second exile came to an end. For the third time in history, Israel became a free and independent nation, speaking the same language, bearing the same name, upholding the same faith, and occupying the same land that it had occupied three thousand years ago.

2

AN ANCIENT PROPHECY
FULFILLED

THE TALMUD SAYS, "As the olive tree has its future in the end, so too has Israel." After two thousand years of waiting, the harvest was about to be realized.

Invitations had been secretly delivered to two hundred leaders among the Jews of Palestine. They were invited to gather at the Municipal Museum in Tel Aviv on the afternoon of May 14, 1948, wearing "festive dark clothes." At sunset the Sabbath would begin, and nothing could be done for another twenty-four hours. Promptly at four P.M. the gathering arose and sang the Zionist hymn—"Hatikvah"—which was to become the Israeli National Anthem.

> So long as still within our breasts
> The Jewish heart beats true.
> So long as still towards the East,
> To Zion looks the Jew,
> So long our hopes are not yet lost—
> Two thousand years we cherished them—
> To live in freedom in the land
> Of Zion and Jerusalem.

David Ben-Gurion, standing beneath a portrait of Theodor Herzl and flanked on either side by the blue Star of David, would for the next seventeen minutes read from a 697-word document. The official English translation of that document, the Proclamation of Independence, in part, reads like this:

> IN THE LAND OF ISRAEL the Jewish people came into being. In this Land was shaped their spiritual, religious and national character. Here they lived in sovereign indepen-

52

dence. Here they created a culture of national and universal import, and gave to the world the eternal Book of Books.

Exiled by force, still the Jewish people kept faith with their Land in all the countries of their dispersion, steadfast in their prayer and hope to return and here revive their political freedom.

Fired by this attachment of history and tradition, the Jews in every generation strove to renew their roots in the ancient Homeland, and in recent generations they came home in their multitudes.

Veteran pioneers and defenders, and newcomers braving blockade, they made the wilderness bloom, revived their Hebrew tongue, and built villages and towns. They founded a thriving society, master of its own economy and culture, pursuing peace but able to defend itself, bringing the blessing of progress to all the inhabitants of the Land, dedicated to the attainment of sovereign independence.

In 1897 the First Zionist Congress met at the call of Theodor Herzl, seer of the vision of the Jewish State, and gave public voice to the right of the Jewish people to national restoration in their Land.

This right was acknowledged in the Balfour Declaration on 2 November 1917 and confirmed in the Mandate of the League of Nations, which accorded international validity to the historical connection between the Jewish people and the Land of Israel, and to their right to re-establish their National Home.

The holocaust that in our time destroyed millions of Jews in Europe again proved beyond doubt the compelling need to solve the problem of Jewish homelessness and dependence by the renewal of the Jewish State in the Land of Israel, which would open wide the gates of the Homeland to every Jew and endow the Jewish people with the status of a nation with equality of rights within the family of nations.

Despite every hardship, hindrance and peril, the remnant that survived the grim Nazi slaughter in Europe, together with Jews from other countries, pressed on with their exodus to the Land of Israel and continued to assert their right to a life of dignity, freedom and honest toil in the Homeland of their people.

In the Second World War, the Jewish community in the Land of Israel played its full part in the struggle of the nations championing freedom and peace against the Nazi forces of evil. Its war effort and the lives of its soldiers won it the right to be numbered among the founding peoples of the United Nations.

On 29 November 1947 the General Assembly of the United Nations adopted a resolution calling for the establishment of a Jewish State in the Land of Israel, and required the inhabitants themselves to take all measures necessary on their part to carry out the resolution. This recognition by the United Nations of the right of the Jewish people to establish their own State is irrevocable.

It is the natural right of the Jewish people, like any other people, to control their own destiny in their sovereign State.

ACCORDINGLY WE, the members of the National Council, representing the Jewish people in the Land of Israel and the Zionist Movement, have assembled on the day of the termination of the British Mandate for Palestine, and, by virtue of our natural and historic right and of the resolution of the General Assembly of the United Nations, do hereby proclaim the establishment of a Jewish State in the Land of Israel—the State of Israel.

WE RESOLVE that, from the moment the Mandate ends, at midnight on the Sabbath, the sixth of Iyar 5708, the fifteenth day of May 1948, until the establishment of the duly elected authorities of the State in accordance with a Constitution to be adopted by the Elected Constituent Assembly not later than 1 October 1948, the National Council shall act as the Provisional Council of State, and its executive arm, the National Administration, shall constitute the Provisional Government of the Jewish State, and the name of that State shall be Israel.

THE STATE OF ISRAEL will be open to Jewish immigration and the ingathering of exiles. It will devote itself to developing the Land for the good of all its inhabitants.

It will rest upon foundations of liberty, justice and peace as envisioned by the Prophets of Israel. It will maintain complete equality of social and political rights for all its citizens, without distinction of creed, race or sex. It will guarantee freedom of religion and conscience, of language, education and culture. It will safeguard the Holy Places of all religions. It will be loyal to the principles of the United Nations Charter. . . .

WITH TRUST IN THE ROCK OF ISRAEL, we set our hands in witness to this Proclamation, at this session of the Provisional Council of State, on the soil of the Homeland, in the city of Tel Aviv, this Sabbath eve, the fifth day of Iyar, 5708, the fourteenth day of May, nineteen hundred and forty-eight.

In the midst of the reading of the Proclamation of Independence, David Ben-Gurion was interrupted with a wild storm of applause when he read the words, "The State of Israel will be open to Jewish immigration and the ingathering of exiles." With these words, the hated British White Paper of 1939, which severely restricted Jewish immigration, was annulled. From May 15 until the end of that year, 101,828 immigrants would enter Israel. The next year, 1949, would see the largest number ever to immigrate—239,576 people. The right of every Jew to live in the Holy Land is a fundamental principle of the State of Israel. Besides being written into the Proclamation of Independence, it was given statutory sanction by the Law of Return, passed by the Knesset on July 5, 1950. Since that time, Israel has welcomed over one and one-quarter million Jews home to the land. With the return of each new immigrant to Israel, we are seeing further fulfillment of many Old Testament prophecies which predict that the Jews will return to the land just prior to the reign of the Messiah.

The remarkable prophecy of Theodor Herzl was fulfilled—the State of Israel had come into being, fifty years and nine months after Herzl had predicted that it would. At 6:11 p.m. Washington time, President Truman issued the following statement: "This Government has been informed that a Jewish State has been proclaimed in Palestine. . . . The United States recognizes the Provisional Government as the de facto authority of the new State of Israel." This was eleven minutes after midnight Israel time, May 15, 1948. Three days later, the Soviet Union gave official recognition to the government of Israel. These events made the State of Israel an historic fact. The Roman emperor Hadrian had once said to Rabbi Joshua, "You are among us as a lamb among seventy wolves. Are we not to be commended for not consuming you?" Rabbi Joshua replied, "It is not your goodness that saves us, but the fact that we have a great shepherd as our guardian." And now, the great Shepherd has returned Israel to the fold! The lamp snuffed out at Bether nearly two thousand years ago had been relighted. It was up to the *Yishuv*—the Jews in the land—to keep it lighted, for on May 15, 1948, with the first light of dawn, the Egyptian Air Force bombed Tel Aviv. The Egyptian Army also crossed Israel's border. The next day the armies of Syria and Lebanon invaded Israel from the north, while the Iraquis came into Israel from the east. The Transjordan Legions were already in Israel. This force was soon joined by those of Saudi Arabia. For the next eight months the new state of Israel was engaged in a war on all fronts.

When David Ben-Gurion had finished reading the Declaration of the Establishment of the State, the gathered assembly wept as the Israel Philharmonic played the Zionist hymn in the background. Aged Rabbi Moshe Fishman said the *Shehecheyanu*, which is a benediction prayed on very special occasions, "Blessed art Thou, O Lord our God, King of the Universe, who has kept us in life, and preserved us and enabled us to reach this season." The delegates emerged from the ceremonial hall, soon to hear the sounds of air-raid sirens and falling bombs which gave reality to the Arab threat.

In just a few hours the Jews could lose two thousand years of hope and anticipation. Abdul Rahman Azzam Pasha, the secretary general of the Arab League had said, "This will be a war of extermination and a momentous massacre which will be spoken of like the Mongol massacres and the Crusades." The Grand Mofti exclaimed: "I declare a holy war, my Moslem brothers! Murder the Jews! Murder them all." Declared Sheikh Hasan el Banna of the Moslem Brotherhood, "All Arabs shall arise and annihilate the Jews! We shall fill the sea with their corpses." In 1948 the Arab menace was deadly serious, for in those days the Arab threat of massacre was a real option for the new state. Israel's population of 650,000 faced a potential united force of forty-five million Arabs, closing in on three sides while Israel's back was to the sea. The Arab League—Egypt, Iraq, Saudi Arabia, Syria, Yemen, Lebanon, and Transjordan—occupied a territory spread over three million square miles, which contained a people thirty times more populous, and a territory two hundred times larger than Palestine. An editorial in Cairo's *Al Kulta* said, "Five hundred thousand Iraquis prepare for this holy war. One hundred fifty thousand Syrians will storm over the Palestine borders and the mighty Egyptian army will throw the Jews into the sea if they dare to declare their state." Commenting sometime later on the general situation, Golda Meir said, "We intend to remain alive. Our neighbors want to see us dead. This is not a question which leaves much room for compromise!"

British Field Marshal Montgomery concurred with the precarious plight of Israel, for he had recently visited Palestine to evaluate the forthcoming military situation. In a report, he wrote that it would take the Arabs eight to ten days to drive the Jews into the sea. The territory that the Jews had to defend was long and skinny. It was almost all border, surrounded on three sides by enemy nations. Militarily, it was indefensible. Paradoxically, twenty years later, when the Six Day War was over, Israel would be in control of a territory three times larger, but with frontiers only half as long as those in 1948!

On May 15, 1948, the aspirations of political Zionism were fulfilled. Herzl had summed up the Jewish problem and its solution thus: "Let the sovereignty be granted us over a portion of the globe large enough to satisfy the rightful requirements of a nation, the rest we will manage ourselves."[1] After the new state's sovereignty was granted, Israel did manage, but against odds that would have overwhelmed a less determined people. However, political Zionism had become almost a Messianic project in the minds of many Jews by this time.

Looking back over Herzl's fifty years for fulfillment, between 1897 and 1947, there are several great events in Zionism whose tributaries merge to form the new State of Israel.

The first of these great events in Zionism is the First Zionist Congress itself, held in Basel, in August, 1897, eighteen months after Herzl had published *The Jewish State*. The First Zionist Congress was composed of 204 delegates from Europe, Africa, America, and Palestine. It was the first meeting of universal Jewry since the Great Revolt nearly two thousand years earlier. The Congress did four things. First, it endowed the people with a living zeal for a return to the land, transforming the latent hope for reunion with the land into a living and aggressive anticipation. When the fiftieth anniversary of the First Zionist Congress was held in Jerusalem in August, 1947, fifteen of the original delegates were present for the celebration. Professor Joseph Klausner of Hebrew University, recalling the thrill of the First Zionist Congress, declared that Herzl had created something hardly expressible in words; something totally new had come into being. In the heart of every one of the 204 delegates burned a spark of Herzl's fire. This First Congress also gave Zionism a platform: "The aim of Zionism is to create a publicly recognized, legally secured home for the Jewish people in Palestine." In addition, the Congress gave birth to the Jewish flag, featuring broad stripes of blue and white with a Star of David in the center. The inspiration for this flag seems to have come from the Jewish prayer shawl. The fourth asset to emerge from the Congress was the Zionist anthem, "Hatikvah" (The Hope). The source of its melody, which combines pathos and victory, is unknown. The words were written by Naphtali Herz Imber, a Hebrew poet.

During the Congress, Theodor Herzl informed the delegates that they were present in Basel "to lay the foundations for the edifice which is one day to house the Jewish people." He saw the doorway to this house even then in existence, for he described current Zionism as "a return to the Jewish fold even before it becomes a return to the Jewish land." The goal of the congress was "the transformation of the Jewish question into a question of Zion," for no solution to the misery of the Jew would be permanent without a land of refuge. A few years later, Max Nordau, who had also addressed the First Zionist Congress, gave a definition of this new Zionism. "The New Zionism, which has been called political, differs from the old, religious, messianic variety in that it disavows all mysticism, no longer identifies itself with messianism, and does not expect the return to Palestine to be brought about by a miracle, but desires to prepare the way by its own efforts."² These efforts were to be fourfold: (1) The systematic promotion of the settlement of Palestine by Jewish farmers, laborers and artisans; (2) the organization of Jewry into local and general bodies in conformity with the laws of their respective countries; (3) the strengthening of Jewish sentiment and national consciousness; (4) the initiation of steps to obtain such government assents as may be necessary for achieving the aim of Zionism. These were the measures which would be taken in order to realize the aim of Zionism—to create a publicly recognized, legally secured home for the Jewish people in Palestine.

Even before the publication of Herzl's *The Jewish State*, and the convening of the First Zionist Congress in Basel, in 1897, a second significant factor in the creation of the new State of Israel had occurred. This was the first of the aliyahs.

During the years of the second exile from the land, Palestine had become more and more denuded—an eroded wilderness. It had been occupied by a succession of invaders and conquerors, in an alien suzerainty which stretched from the fall of Bethar in A.D. 135 to the modern era. Palestine never became a permanent homeland for any people. It was conquered and reconquered fourteen times in thirteen centuries. Roman and Byzantine rule lasted for five hundred years. In A.D. 614 the Persians came, only to be followed by the Arabs (673-1072), Seljurks (1072-1099), Crusaders (1099-1291), Mamluks (1291-1517), and Ottoman Turks (1517-1917).

But at no time during all these eras was Palestine completely free of Jewish inhabitants. In fact, though the Roman conquests of the first and second centuries drove thousands of Jews from the land, Jews probably remained the predominant population for several centuries after the Great Revolt. However, Jewish population persistently declined over the years. On occasions it was increased by immigration, due to periodic reverses of the Jewish situation in Europe. However, prior to 1882 the only constant immigration to Palestine comprised Orthodox Jews who returned to the land for religious reasons.

The first aliyah was made up largely of Russian immigrants fleeing the pograms. *Aliyah* in Hebrew means "going up." It is a term used for those returning to the homeland. *Aliyah* is used in the synagogue when one is called up to read from the Torah. It also refers to the honor bestowed upon one in the synagogue who is chosen to open and close the Torah ark where the scrolls are kept. To participate in the synagogue aliyah is a great privilege for the Jewish worshiper. *Aliyah* was also applied to those making the journey up to Jerusalem to celebrate the great pilgrim feasts of Passover, Pentecost, and the Feast of Tabernacles. Since it was used of the Jews who returned from the first exile in Babylon, it was only natural to apply this sacred term to those returning Jews going up to the land from the scattering of the second exile.

The first aliyah covers the years 1882-1903. Nearing Jaffa harbor on August 11, 1882, a first wave of immigrants drew up a Jewish Mayflower Compact in which they envisioned an agriculturally oriented, corporate society, based on the ideal for the rebirth of Israel. During the first aliyah, as many intended sending out teachers and builders to establish other colonies. However, their first few years were years of privation, spiritual anguish, starvation, and neglect. The group was composed largely of young idealists—college students—who had no training in agriculture, or little else for that matter. They were sustained only by their passionate ideal for the rebirth of Israel. During the first aliyah, as many as thirty agricultural colonies may have been settled in Palestine. By 1903 there were sixty thousand Jews living in the land.

The first aliyah was characterized by the self-sacrificing idealism of its immigrants. The second aliyah, between 1903 and 1914, was characterized by a labor philosophy. Aaron David Gordon had influenced many European intellectuals with a philosophy of labor which he believed was the needed ingredient in the establishment of the new state. He wrote in 1911, "The Jewish people have been completely cut off from nature and imprisoned within city walls for two thousand years. We have become accustomed to every form of life, except to a life of labor—of labor done at our own behest and for its own sake. It will require the greatest effort of will for such a people to become normal again. We lack the principal ingredient for national life. We lack the habit of labor—not labor performed out of external compulsion, but labor in which one is attached in a natural and organic way. This kind of labor binds a people to its soil and to its natural culture, which in turn is an outgrowth of the people's soil and the people's labor."[3]

The philosophy of Aaron David Gordon became the format for the new Jewish immigration. David Ben-Gurion and Levi Eshkol were among these labor pioneers. Both the *kibbutz* and the *Haganah* grew out of the labor movement also. The kibbutz was the corporate settlement in which immigrant Jews united their toil in common effort to survive. The Haganah emerged as the root of the modern Israeli army because of the need of common defense. By the eve of the First World War there were ninety thousand Jews in Palestine living on forty-five agricultural settlements in addition to the large cities.

Though the kibbutz was conceived during the second aliyah, it was during the third aliyah, following the First World War (1919-1925), that the kibbutz really thrived, with thousands of young Jews working as laborers in agricultural camps. Swamps were drained, roads were paved, land was reclaimed, forests were planted. This was also an era of organizational advance. It was during these years that a real basis was laid for a future national life. The Jewish population by 1925 was officially estimated at 108,000.

The fourth aliyah occurred between 1925 and 1932. Its main impetus was thousands of Jews who were forced to leave Poland. As many as sixty-two thousand Jews may have come to Palestine in a two-year period due to the reforms of the minister of finance, which excluded the Polish Jew from any meaningful participation in commerce. Consequently, this wave of immigrants was composed largely of middle-aged, middle-class, East European Jews. They were merchantmen and factory workers who had no previous experience in agriculture. Tel Aviv, which was established in 1909, as a suburb of Jaffa, became the commercial, industrial, and cultural center of Palestine. Daily newspapers appeared in Hebrew during this time. Theaters also presented plays in Hebrew, while the Palestine Symphony Orchestra performed, directed by Arturo Toscanini.

The fifth aliyah beginning in the early 1930's swelled Palestine's Jewish population with immigrants fleeing the pre-World War II Nazi persecutions. It was German-speaking intellectuals who came during these years making important contributions to agriculture, business, industry, economics, science, and the professions. Many of these brilliant professional people gave a great boost to medicine, education, engineering, hygiene, the law, and many other areas of practical need. Culture was enhanced by many artists who had been expelled as a result of Nazi oppression. At one time, during 1936, the Palestine Symphony Orchestra had no less than four first violins who had been expelled from imminent European orchestras. Because many of these skilled professionals and intellectuals could not be utilized in their own fields, they became farmers. Soon their brilliance had effected the efficiency of agriculture. Economic life was also infused with a new dynamic by the army of bankers and industrialists driven from Germany. The Hebrew University, founded earlier, became a great institution of higher learning during this aliyah. At the beginning of World War II the Jewish population of Palestine had reached half a million, which constituted about thirty percent of the total population.

The fifth aliyah was followed by an era of illegal immigration, between 1940 and 1948. During the Second World War, the British government clamped down on immigration. While thousands of Jews were dying in the concentration camps of Germany, Great Britain contributed to their helpless plight by refusing them admission into Palestine. The British White Paper, issued May 17, 1939, had stated, "His Majesty's Government therefore now declares unequivocally that it is not part of their policy that Palestine should become a Jewish State." Two restrictions put teeth into this decision. First, Jews could purchase land in only a designated five percent of Palestine. Second, during the next five years only seventy-five thousand Jews could immigrate. After five years no further Jewish immigration would be permitted unless the Arabs of Palestine agreed. Thus in five years Palestine would be closed to the Jews, for the Arabs would never agree to more immigration. The tragedy of the British White Paper is that it came at a time when millions of Jews were being persecuted in Europe and were seeking to flee the coming holocaust. Golda Meir, in formulating the official Zionist answer, protested that in the darkest hour of Jewish history, the British government deprived the Jews of their last hope when they closed the road back to their homeland. However, even in the face of these restrictions, it is estimated that 140,000 Jews did get in—many by illegal means. This era is sometimes called "the blockade-running aliyah."

These six aliyoth made inevitable the momentous events of 1947-1948. After World War II ended, there were hundreds of thousands of Jews, survivors of the Nazi horror, who were clamoring for admission into Palestine. The British could no longer hold them out, and therefore in 1947 Great Britain brought the Palestine question to the United Nations for a solution.

The Balfour Declaration is another mountain peak in the fifty year struggle of Zionism. In 1917 the British army liberated Palestine from a Turkish rule which had lasted for four hundred years—since Sultan Selim took Palestine from the Mameluke rulers of Egypt in 1517. After the First World War ended, in 1922 the British government was given a mandate by the League of Nations to administer Palestine. A part of the League of Nations Mandate for Palestine, under which Britain was to govern the land, was the explicit recognition of the historical connection between the Jewish people and the land, and the implications of this for the reconstruction of the Jewish national home in that country. That the Jews were there "as a right and not on sufferance," was the British statement of policy recognized by the British colonial secretary, Winston Churchill. An inseparable part of the League of Nations' Mandate was the Balfour Declaration, which had been issued in 1917. The issuance of this declaration was the third great event in political Zionism.

The Jews were sympathetic to the Allied cause in the First World War. Zionist designs for the restoration of Palestine as a homeland for the Jews increased as a hopeful option when the Turks entered the Great War on the side of Germany. After this, an Allied victory over Germany and Turkey would erase the problem of Turkish opposition to Zionism.

For centuries one of the Allied countries, France, had indicated an interest in Palestine, based largely upon the fact that most of the Crusaders were French. When the Allies had defeated Germany and Turkey, France might conceivably lay claim to Palestine. Therefore, in order to preclude any French claim to Palestine when World War I was over, the British backed the Zionist cause and issued the Balfour Declaration in 1917.

It came about like this. Author James Balfour had met the future president of the State of Israel, Chaim Weizmann, in 1906. Lord Balfour had wanted to persuade the Zionists that they were wrong in turning down Great Britain's offer of territory in Uganda for a national home. Instead, Balfour was convinced by Weizmann that Palestine was the only suitable homeland for the Jews. During the First World War, Weizmann, who was a brilliant chemist, helped the British government solve some problems in the production of acetone. By this he gained a friend in Lloyd George, who was to become prime minister of Great Britain, and in whose cabinet Lord Balfour served as foreign minister.

In January, 1917, Weizmann submitted to the British Foreign Office his Outline of Program for the Jewish Resettlement of Palestine in Accordance with the Aspirations of the Zionist Movement. The program contended for the Jews in Palestine to be recognized as a nation and to be accorded attendant rights as a free nation, including the right to purchase land in Palestine and to immigrate. When President Woodrow Wilson indicated that the United States government would support the declaration, the British Foreign Office issued on November 2, 1917, the following declaration:

> His Majesty's Government views with favor the establishment in Palestine of a national home for the Jewish people, and will use their best endeavours to facilitate the achievement of this object, it being clearly understood that nothing shall be done which may prejudice the civil and religious rights of existing non-Jewish communities in Palestine, or the

rights and political status enjoyed by Jews in any other country.

Though the Jewish people were soon to become disillusioned with the Balfour Declaration, it would be cited as the legal basis of the appeal for Jewish statehood which the representatives of the Jewish Agency would use as they effectively pled their case before the United Nations Special Committee on Palestine in 1947.

The fourth great victory for Zionism during the half century between 1897 and the birth of Israel, was the action of the United Nations taken in November, 1947. The League of Nations, which had given the British a mandate to govern Palestine, ceased to exist at the outbreak of World War II. The British could neither administer the country internally because of the conflict with the *Yishuv*, those Jewish settlers already in the land, nor stem the tide of immigrants who wanted to enter the land—many of whom were already pouring in illegally. Therefore, on April 2, 1947, the British asked that the Palestine question be placed on the agenda of the United Nations.

When the General Assembly met to consider the question, it was obvious that the Arabs had a clear voice in the proceedings, through their member nations, while the Jews did not. As a result of this imbalance, the United Nations then admitted representatives of the Jewish Agency to state their case before the General Assembly. As a result of these hearings, the General Assembly appointed the United Nations Special Committee on Palestine (UNSCOP).While the Arabs held the threat of war over the committee, the Jewish cause was pled by Dr. Abba Hillel Silver, David Ben-Gurion, and Moshe Sharett. The Jewish case was based largely upon the legal commitments of the Balfour Declaration and the League of Nations' Mandate for Palestine, both of which proposed the establishment of the State of Israel.

The United Nations committee hearing the case adjourned to Palestine to investigate the situation first-hand. While they were there, the Exodus 1947 occurred, in which a shipload of refugees were forcibly returned to Europe after a battle with the British authorities in Haifa. This incident was actually witnessed by some of the UNSCOP members who were in Haifa at the time. The plight of the wretched immigrants who were forced to return to the displaced persons camps of Hamburg served to underscore the failure of the mandate under which Britain was still attempting to govern Palestine.

The United Nations Special Committee on Palestine retired to Geneva and drew up a recommendation that the mandate be ended, and then advocated the partition of Palestine and the creation of statehood for Israel. Fifty-seven percent of Palestine would go to the Jews—in spite of the fact that within this territory two-thirds of the population and more than half of the land was Arab. The Arabs owned more land in this Jewish state than the Jews did! They also recommended a separate enclave for Jerusalem which would be placed under the supervision of the UN Trusteeship Council.

On November 29, 1947, by a 33-to-13 vote (ten abstentions), the United Nations General Assembly passed a resolution on the partition of Palestine. The next day Arab hostilities broke out against the Jews in Palestine, hoping by terrorism to undermine the United Nations decision to create the State of Israel. Though the British were still responsible for the peace of the area, they did little to aid the embattled Jews, indicating a pro-Arab attitude throughout the whole affair. The following May the British withdrew, leaving the country in chaos. In the midst of this hositlity from without, and the chaos within, the new State of Israel was born in May, 1948; with seemingly little chance to survive.

All over the world Jews were jubilant. In most places the rejoicing was evident in public ceremony. A vast gathering was held in Madison Square Garden in New York City with an impressive array of speakers. However, Golda Meir had an experience some weeks later that was less spectacular but indicative of the depth of emotion stirred by the new state. Mrs. Meir's first official position with the new State of Israel was that of Minister to Russia. On her first Saturday in Moscow, she attended a Jewish synagogue. Although a concerted effort had been made to stamp out Judaism in Russia, there were a few synagogues left, attended by a handful of elderly Jews. Leaving the synagogue, she walked toward the Hotel Metropole. An old man passed her and muttered in Yiddish, "Don't talk to me. I'll walk ahead." When the hotel was in sight, he turned to her and said in Hebrew, "Blessed are we that we have lived to see this day." He then disappeared.

Theodor Herzl's prediction, made fifty years before, was fulfilled. However, his prediction about the restoration of the State of Israel was no more than an educated guess. The fact that it came true within nine months of the time limit he placed upon it in 1897 is a matter of coincidence. Everyone recognizes this. But there are dozens of predictions about the regathering of the Jews back to the land and the creation of a new State of Israel which are not the product of conjecture. They are contained in the Old Testament Scriptures and were made twenty-five centuries ago by Hebrew prophets who spoke and wrote under the inspiration of the Spirit of God. It is these Hebrew prophecies about the regathering of Israel whose fulfillment we are witnessing—at least in their initial stages—in our own day.

This great body of Old Testament prophecy which has to do with the coming of the Redeemer and the future of the nation Israel we call Messianic prophecy. While the New Testament tells us *who* the Messiah is, it is the Old Testament that tells us *what* the Messiah is. And *what* the Messiah is, is almost always presented in association with the nation Israel. Though the Old Testament concedes that the Messianic kingdom will include the Gentile nations in its fringe benefits, it is the elect nation Israel which is the focal point of Messianic prophecy in the Old Testament. Therefore, if we recognize that the work of the Messiah, the Lord Jesus Christ, is to bring both Jew and Gentile into a new spiritual relationship with God, as the New Testament teaches, we must also recognize that the nation Israel has a unique place in this redemptive program of God—as the Old Testament teaches.

Messianic prophecy has two dimensions, for there are two distinctive strains of prediction in the Old Testament concerning the coming Messiah. One series of prophecies describes a Messiah who suffers. This is found in Psalm 22, for example. But it is most clearly seen in Isaiah 42:1-4; 49:1-6; 50:4-11; 52:13-53:12. In these suffering Servant poems of Isaiah, there is a movement which at first identifies Israel as the suffering servant. But as the movement continues, a Person who suffers vicariously for the sin of all mankind, finally comes into view—especially in the last Servant poem, 52:13—53:12. A second strain of prophecy sees the Messiah as one who reigns in power and great glory, as in Daniel 7:13-14. So clear and distinctive are these two lines of Messianic prediction that Jewish interpreters long ago proposed the coming of two Messiahs. One they called Messiah Ben Joseph, and the other they called Messiah Ben-David. It is Messiah Ben Joseph who suffers and dies. It is Messiah Ben-David who will reign in great power and glory. However, the Christian expositor recognizes that the prophecies concerning the Messiah are fulfilled in one Person, the Lord Jesus Christ. The prophecies concerning the suffering Servant were fulfilled in the first coming of Christ, while the prophecies concerning the glorious reign of the Messiah will be fulfilled in His second coming.

Now the point is this: As the prophecies concerning the suffering Servant were *literally* fulfilled in the first coming of Christ, just so, the prophecies concerning the glorious reign of the Messiah will be literally fulfilled in the second coming of Christ. But further, since many of the prophecies concerning the glorious reign of the Messiah which will be fulfilled in the second coming of Christ, are made in connection with the restoration and redemption of the nation Israel; it follows that what is predicted of the nation Israel will be literally fulfilled also.

Though the suffering Servant and the reigning King represent the two major themes of Old Testament Messianic prophecy, there is a third facet that is a part of this theme— the Messiah's reign is universal, yet it is inseparably associated with Israel in the land. The imminent Jewish scholar, Professor Klausner, defines Israel's Messianic expectation as "The prophetic hope for the end of this age, in which there will be political freedom, moral perfection, and earthly bliss for the people Israel in its own land, and also for the entire human race."[4] The suffering Servant predictions found literal fulfillment in the first coming of Christ. The reigning Messiah predictions will find literal fulfillment in the second coming of Christ. Since the restoration and redemption of the nation Israel is an inseparable part of the Messiah's reign, as presented in the Old Testament Scriptures, it therefore follows that the promises made to Israel concerning national regathering and redemption must be literally fulfilled also. This is one reason why in Jewish literature the world to come is eschatological while the Messianic age is temporal. Maimonides said, "The final reward and the ultimate good, endless and perfect, is the life of the world to come, but the Days of the Messiah belong to this world, and will be as the world customarily is except that sovereignty will be restored to Israel."

Since most of the Old Testament promises of the regathering of Israel were made in association with the Babylonian crisis and first exile, why were these promises not fulfilled in the return of Israel after the Babylonian captivity in the sixth century B.C.? The answer is that they were fulfilled *partially*, but not *exhaustively*. This means that Old Testament predictive prophecy has the capacity for dual fulfillment. Often there is a partial fulfillment which may take place rather soon after the prediction is made. Many of the prophecies of the return from exile were fulfilled within a century of their utterance. However, the fulfillment was neither permanent nor exhaustive. This means that a further and more distant fulfillment is indicated, which will be both permanent and exhaustive. The return from the first and second exiles have similar characteristics, even though they are separated by twenty-five hundred years—one taking place in the sixth century B.C., while the other occurs in the twentieth century A.D. One was in the near future, while the other was in the distant future. The prophets saw them merged into one event. However, what the prophets predicted about the return of Israel from exile found only a partial fulfillment when Israel returned from Babylon in the sixth century B.C. There awaits an exhaustive fulfillment of these predictions when Israel is fully returned from her recent exile. This is climaxed in association with the second coming of Christ.

The return from Babylonian captivity did not exhaust the things which the prophets predicted would happen when Israel was regathered from exile in the sixth century B.C. Generally the prophets foresaw a glorious future for Israel when she would be returned to the land. However, the restoration from Babylonian exile was inglorious rather than glorious. It took many years to rebuild the temple. The people began the work and then neglected it. Those who remembered the first temple wept because the restored temple was so inferior. The territory which the returning Jews could occupy had been greatly reduced. It involved only a few miles around the city of Jerusalem. The country was filled with hostile people. During the captivity, the surrounding tribes had pushed forward to occupy much of the land which had previously belonged to Judah. The half-idolatrous residents of the northern territory were a heterogeneous mixture of foreign military settlers. All of this, plus a creeping disillusionment, rendered the return from the first exile a demoralizing affair rather than a glorious victory.

The conditions that resulted from the return from the Babylonian exile were generally disappointing; and, specifically, a number of things which the prophets predicted would attend the regathering of Israel from exile just did not happen. Therefore, there was far more prophecy left unfulfilled in the return from the Babylonian exile than there was fulfilled. Either these prophecies of blessings to come upon Israel when she returns to the land were aborted, or they are yet to find fulfillment in association with a future return. And so they will be—when the second coming of Christ completes the regathering of Israel from the second exile.

The preexilian prophets did far more than just prophesy the regathering of scattered Israel. The return of Israel from the first exile in Babylon would have dramatically fulfilled such unadorned and simple predictions. However, the prophecies of Israel's return to the Holy Land, which were given in precise and numerous details, are replete and complex with promised blessings, both spiritual and physical. If the return is to be taken literally, then the attending blessings are also to be taken literally, and we are to expect their fulfillment as well.

Some of the attendant blessings promised to Israel upon her regathering from exile, which were not fulfilled when Israel returned from Babylon, are these:

1. The spiritual regeneration of Israel follows the return to the land (Eze 11:14-21; 36:24-31).
2. The land as well as the people will be transformed (Is 11:6-11).
3. The Messiah will reign following Israel's regathering (Eze 34:23).
4. A permanent sanctuary which will bring glory to God forevermore will be built in their midst (Eze 37:26-28).
5. The Holy Spirit will be poured out upon all Israel (Eze 39:27-29).
6. Israel will be given a new spiritual dynamic which will enable her to walk in the Lord's statutes (Eze 36:26-28).
7. There will be a reunion of Israel and Judah (Eze 37:15-28).
8. A king in the line of David will reign upon the throne (Eze 37:22-24).
9. Israel will dwell in peace and security (Eze 34:27-30).

Not by the wildest application of exegetical ingenuity or stretch of interpretative imagination can these predictions be said to have found fulfillment when Israel returned from the Babylonian exile in the sixth century B.C. The promises which are found in the Old Testament prophets concerning Israel's golden age, to be realized after her regathering back into the land, must await a larger fulfillment as a result of Israel's regathering from the second exile, and in association with the second coming of Christ.

The ancient Hebrew's understanding of himself and his relationship to the world stood upon a triple idealism: individual morality, social justice, and universal peace. The Jews therefore conceived of history in terms of progress— progress toward a golden age, and not away from it.

These agriculturalists on the eastern shores of the Mediterranean Sea developed a uniquely original view of individual *moral choice* which would determine destinies. In the Apocrypha, Ben-Sira said, "God created man. . .and put him in the power of his will" (Ec'us 15:14). Their ideas about the freedom of man's will replaced the fatalism, the determination and the resignation with which most ancients viewed the world of daily events. Instead of the capricious actions of supernatural forces, the Hebrews saw the choice of man as the determinant force in human affairs. Man was not passive, but he was an active agent in the course of history. The Greek viewed history as moving in a circle. But the Hebrews saw it moving in a straight line toward a future goal. They also believed that man's free choice and action within the context of this linear view of history would either hasten or delay the coming golden age. Also, the ideal of Hebrew *social ethic* emerged against the background of human exploitation. The Hebrew prophets contended against their own princes, who would exploit the people, and against their own judges, who would pervert justice. This social justice was a theme of the great eighth century prophets of Israel. The third ideal upon which the Hebrew view of history stood was that of the possibility of *universal peace*. War was not an inexorable part of human destiny. Rather, a golden age of peace lay in the future.

The Jewish people believed themselves to be the responsible custodians of these ideals of moral choice, social justice, and universal peace. In their quest for the realization of these ideals, their progress was interrupted by exile and dispersement. However, the prophets of Israel also taught that even if the quest for these values was interrupted by exile, they would be realized in a future restoration of the nation Israel. Therefore, the doctrine of restoration sustained Israel's hope in the ultimate realization of these unique ideals. This was the theme of the Old Testament prophets who declared that even though Israel defected from the purposes of God, and even though the people were scattered in exile as a consequence of their free moral choice, they would ultimately be regathered and restored. In this restoration to the land they would finally realize this unique dream of individual morality, social justice, and universal peace.

Today this triple ideal still influences the Jewish under-

standing of himself and his place in history; indeed, it per-
vades all mankind as a heritage from ancient Israel. But how
is this ideal to be realized? Both Christians and Jews have
reflected upon this ideal and the method of its fulfillment in
history. And oddly enough, the proposed answer to this
quest does not turn out to be a Christian answer as opposed
to a Jewish answer. Rather, the issue finds its resolution
along lines which pit a liberal-philosophic solution against a
faith-oriented and Scriptural solution.

The liberal-philosophic solution to the problem is represented by those who have retained the ideal of individual
morality, social justice, and universal peace, but have relin-
quished the biblical dynamic for its realization. This group is
composed of Reform Jews and liberal Christians. In their
optimism about the inevitable perfectibility of man, they see
the hope of personal morality, social justice, and universal
peace realized through man's own idealistic efforts. In fact,
Reform Judaism has rejected all the old traditional ideas
about the coming of the Messiah which are found in the Old
Testament, the Talmud, the Midrash, and in the Zohar.

It was in the Napoleonic era, as European Jews were
beginning to feel the security of acceptance, that the Messianic ideals began to wane. As a practical answer to the
Jewish problem, Messianism began to fade after the rash of
false messiahs which had appeared during the preceding
Cabalistic era. Now, during the early nineteenth century,
the Messianic ideal, as a basic doctrine of Judaism, began to
be eroded away by the Reform movement. Based largely
upon the cosmopolitan ideals of the French encyclopedists
and the granting of civil and religious liberties to the Jews by
the French government, Messianic anticipation rapidly subsided from popular Jewish imagination. It lived on mostly
among the Orthodox. In this era was emerging a new generation of Jews which would disavow the hope of Messianic
restoration and replace it with national acceptance and citizenship.

Also during the early nineteenth century, liberal Jewish
voices were urging the innovations which have become so
familiar in Reform Judaism. The Hebrew language and the
Messianic hope were chief among the objects of the reform-

ers ambivalence. Jews should love the land that gives to them citizenship, and they should worship in the language of that country, not in Hebrew. The Messianic hope, with its attendant hope of restoration to the land, should be abandoned, and all Jews should find their aspirations fulfilled in acceptance and assimilation among the people of their present home, said the Reformers in Judaism. Though the Messianic elements were not immediately expurgated from the traditional prayer book, they were soon to be interpreted as symbols. However, by mid-nineteenth century in Germany, all references to Zion and Jerusalem, to the coming of the Messiah, and to the resurrection of the dead, had been omitted from the Reform Prayer Book. The heart of the contention lay in the belief held by the newly emancipated Jew that the Messianic hope, along with his attendant anticipation of a Jewish return to their homeland, was a contradiction to the Jews' newfound acceptance as a citizen of the European community. Citizenship demanded a corresponding loyalty to the country which had accepted the Jew as a citizen. But this stood in inherent contradiction to Messianic Zionism. Later, the Reform Jew would reject political Zionism for the same reason.

It is true that the rosy optimism of the liberal Christian has been radically shaken by the events of the twentieth century. They are having second thoughts about the spark of deity which they declared to be inherent in every man, and the inevitability of human moral progress which they believed would lead to a golden age. The liberal Christian entered the twentieth century believing that this would indeed be *the* Christian century. Smitten with an evolutionary philosophy which he believed would cause the inherent goodness of man to triumph shortly, the liberal theologian was completely demoralized by two world wars, the Nazi holocaust, the two succeeding conflicts in Korea and Vietnam, along with the threat of an atomic climax to history. Classic modernism faded away in the aftermath of these events, which gave conclusive testimony that the Bible was correct all the while—man is a hopeless sinner and, apart from the cross of Jesus Christ, is incapable of extirpating himself from the moral mess he has made of things. Reform Jews, however, whose new optimistic philosophy and idealistic hope are not as likely to be shattered by the events of the last few decades, still believe that these ideals will prevail. But even today the sterile utopianism of Reform Judaism is being tested, for most of the Jewish young people who are coming to know the Lord Jesus Christ as personal Saviour and Messiah are coming out of the vapid atmosphere of Reform Judaism.

In contrast to Reform Jews and liberal Christians, who hold the ideal but have rejected the biblical method of realizing the ideal, is a second group which still retains the biblical hope of individual morality, social justice, and universal peace. But they also retain the biblical method of realizing this hope. Both Orthodox Jews and evangelical Christians believe that these ideals of moral perfection, social equity and world peace can only be fully realized by eschatological means—the coming of the Messiah into human history. While Orthodox Jews still await an only coming of the Messiah, evangelical Christians anticipate the second coming of the Lord Jesus Christ who alone can usher in the golden age of peace, justice, and righteousness.

However, the evangelical Christian's hope of righteousness, social justice, and universal peace, which is related to the return of the Messiah, the Lord Jesus Christ, does not exclude the restoration of the nation Israel in its context. The realization of these ideals and the restoration of the nation Israel are inseparable in the teaching of the Old Testament prophets. The Messiah will produce universal righteousness, justice, and peace when He comes. But the consistent testimony of Scripture is that the Messiah will produce them only in relationship to His reign on earth over regathered and regenerated Israel. This is the prophetic frame of reference that we must retain if we are to rightly divide the Word of Truth.

The prophet Isaiah says,

> And it shall come to pass in that day, that the Lord will set his hand again the second time to recover the remnant of his people, that shall remain. . . .And he will set up an ensign for the nations, and will assemble the outcasts of Israel, and gather together the dispersed of Judah from the four corners

of the earth (11:11-12; cf. 12:1-3; 27:12-13; 43:1-8; 49:8-16;
66:20-22).

The prophet Jeremiah says,

> Therefore, behold, the days come, saith the LORD, that it
> shall no more be said, As the LORD liveth, that brought up the
> children of Israel out of the land of Egypt; but, As the LORD
> liveth, that brought up the children of Israel from the land of
> the north and from all the countries whither he had driven
> them. And I will bring them again into their land that I gave
> unto their fathers (Jer 16:14-15; cf. 23:3-8; 30:10-11; 31:8).

The prophet Ezekiel says,

> For thus saith the Lord GOD: Behold, I myself, even I, will
> search for my sheep, and will seek them out. As a shepherd
> seeketh out his flock in the day that he is among his sheep that
> are scattered abroad, so will I seek out my sheep; and I will
> deliver them out of all places whither they have been scat-
> tered in the cloudy and dark day. And I will bring them out
> from the peoples, and gather them from the countries, and
> will bring them into their own land; and I will feed them upon
> the mountains of Israel, by the watercourses, and in all the
> inhabited places of the country (Eze 34:11-13; cf. 11:17-21;
> 20:33-38; 39:25-29).

The prophet Amos says,

> And I will bring back the captivity of my people Israel, and
> they shall build the waste cities, and inhabit them; and they
> shall plant vineyards, and drink the wine thereof; they shall
> also make gardens, and eat the fruit of them. And I will plant
> them upon their land, and they shall no more be plucked up
> out of their land which I have given them, saith the LORD thy
> God (Amos 9:14-15).

The prophet Zechariah says,

> Thus saith the LORD of hosts: There shall yet old men and old
> women dwell in the streets of Jerusalem, every man with his
> staff in his hand for very age. And the streets of the city shall
> be full of boys and girls playing in the streets thereof. Thus
> saith the LORD of hosts: If it be marvellous in the eyes of the
> remnant of this people in those days, should it also be mar-

vellous in mine eyes? saith the LORD of hosts. Thus saith the LORD of hosts: Behold, I will save my people from the east country, and from the west country; and I will bring them, and they shall dwell in the midst of Jerusalem; and they shall be my people, and I will be their God, in truth and in righteousness (Zec 8:4-8).

For the first time in nearly two thousand years, the Jews are back in the land in their own sovereign state. Is this then the fulfillment of what these prophets have predicted about the restoration of the nation Israel in the last days?

The answer is both yes and no.

The answer is no in the sense that Israel, though back in the land, has not fully realized all the coordinate blessings that the prophets indicated would surround the return. These blessings are both physical and spiritual (cf. Amos 9:11-14; Eze 11:17-21). Obviously these predictions have not as yet been fulfilled, nor will they be fulfilled until the second coming of Christ.

But the answer to the question is also yes, for the Old Testament prophets taught that the initial ingathering would take place while Israel is still in unbelief. These prophecies about the restoration of Israel while the nation is still in unbelief may very well find fulfillment in the contemporary State of Israel.

The most famous Old Testament prediction about the return of Israel to the land, which also confirms that that return will initially take place while the Jew is still in the rejection of Jesus as Messiah, is Ezekiel's vision of the valley of dry bones, found in chapter 37.

It is obvious that Ezekiel's version was not fulfilled when Israel returned from the first exile in Babylon for the reasons that we have already pointed out—the attending promises of physical and spiritual blessings were just not realized when Israel returned to the land in the sixth century B.C. In verses 15-28 of this same chapter, Ezekiel indicates a number of things that will happen as a result of the dry bones living again. Judah and Israel will be reunited (vv. 15-22); they will not be defiled with any more transgressions (v. 23); a King from the royal house of David will reign over them forever

(vv. 24-25); they will walk in the ordinances and obey the Lord's statutes (v. 24); their dwelling in the land will be permanent, for they will never again be removed from off the land (v. 25); they will dwell under an everlasting covenant of peace (v. 26); and the temple will be permanently restored as a testimony to all the nations that the Lord has sanctified Israel. None of these happened as a result of the return from Babylonian exile.

But note. Though these glorious blessings will come to pass as a result of Israel's return to the land, during the first stages of the return they will not be realized, for Israel returns in a state of unbelief. God's order of events surrounding the return of Israel is first *regathering*, next *regeneration*, then full *restoration*. Their spiritual regeneration and the restoration of former blessings will not occur until Israel is first regathered. It is obvious then that if Israel is not regenerated until after she is back in the land, the initial return to the land must occur while the Jews are still in the rejection of the Lord Jesus Christ. This is why Ezekiel saw the events occur in their particular sequence.

First he saw a valley of dry bones, 37:1-3. The fact that they were very dry underscores the desperate plight of the nation Israel while in exile. There follows the question which both Jews and Christians have asked for the last two thousand years, "Can these bones live?" Is there a future for the nation Israel in the plan of God? During all those centuries, while Israel was scattered across the face of the earth, both Orthodox Jews and premillennial Christians maintained the biblical anticipation that Israel would live again as a nation in the land.

Next, it is significant that the bones come together in the context of a noise and earthquake, (v. 7). Perhaps this is a picture of modern anti-Semitism which climaxed in the shaking events of the Nazi holocaust. That tragedy finally awakened the entire world to the Jewish need for a national homeland.

Then the bones are gathered together, but, "there was no breath in them" (v. 8). This is a picture of Israel in the land today. They have been assembled, but there is no Spirit in them (v. 9). They have been gathered back to the land in unbelief. There, though they know it not, regathered Israel now awaits the second coming of Christ which will breathe spiritual life into them (cf. 36:24-31).

The fact that Israel is regathered back to the land in unbelief and then experiences spiritual regeneration is set forth in many other passages which deal with the return. One such passage is Deuteronomy 30:5-6. Here regeneration follows regathering. The same sequence can be found in Ezekiel 11:17-20 and 36:24-27.

In all of these passages, spiritual regeneration does not *precede*, but *follows* the return to the land. Therefore, the biblical order is: Israel regathered in unbelief, followed by spiritual regeneration taking place while Israel is already in the land. It does not precede the return to the land.

It is at this point that Christian and rabbinical views of the return differ. Evangelical Christians, who take the prophetic Scriptures both seriously and literally, hold the view of the Old Testament prophets: spiritual righteousness follows regathering. However, the rabbinic view is that spiritual righteousness must precede regathering.

The Orthodox Jewish view is that Israel ushers in the age of the Messiah by her own righteousness. A very famous Hasidic parable presents this notion. A migratory bird of rare beauty flew past the royal palace and alighted on the top of a high palm tree. The king yearned to possess this beautiful creature and instructed his courtiers to form a human ladder, one to stand on the shoulders of the other, until the highest could throw a net upon the bird. Though only men of strength were chosen, one weakened, and the entire human structure collapsed to the ground. By virtue of one man's fault, the king's desire could not be fulfilled. It is the same with us, say the Hasidic rabbis. The man of holiness depends upon the support of a lesser man, and the latter depends upon men of even lower quality in order to attain the summit of holiness and to bring down God's love. But when one person weakens, the whole structure totters and falls, and the whole process must begin anew.

This idea of universal Jewish righteousness as a prerequisite to the Messiah's coming began to take shape after numerous rabbinic calculations for the time of the Messiah's advent had failed. After many dates which had been set for the Messiah's coming failed to work out, the advent of the Messiah was then made dependent upon Israel's righteousness.

Indications of the idea are found throughout the Talmud and the Midrash. Rabbi Simon Ben-Yohai said, "If Israel were to keep two Sabbaths according to the laws thereof, they would be redeemed immediately!" Rabbi Jose said, "Great is charity in that it brings the redeemer nearer." Rabbi Jose the Galileean said, "Great is repentance because it brings near redemption." The rabbis taught, "proselytes and those that play with children delay the Messiah." The Gemara explains, "Those that play with children" are those who marry girls too young to bear children, and the proselytes which delay the Messiah's coming are those not scrupulous enough in keeping the commandments. The rabbis had said, "Israel will not be redeemed until all the children of Israel are united in a single fellowship." The Talmud declared, "The Son of David will not come until all evil judges will cease out of Israel," and "The Son of David will not come until the arrogant cease out of Israel." Rabbi Tanhum, son of Rabbi Hiyya, said, "The King-Messiah will not come until all the souls which it was originally the divine intention to create shall have come to an end." After the fall of the second temple, marriage was neglected because of persecution. Especially was this true after the revolt of Bar Kokhba and the persecutions of Hadrian. The Roman emperor issued an edict forbidding the observance of the Torah, and therefore children could not be circumcised. The rabbis said that it was better not to marry and thus have no children, than to have them and not be able to circumcise them. This delayed the Messiah's advent, say the rabbis.

However, this idea persisted long after the Talmudic period. There is even a year known to Jewish historians as "the year of penitence" which occurred in the sixteenth century. In 1502 a German Jew named Asher Lämmlein, encouraged by the Messianic predictions of certain of his contemporaries, declared himself as the forerunner of the Messiah. He went about preaching that if the Jews would spend six months in repentance and chastisement and in doing good works, the Messiah would appear. He would be preceded by a column of fire and a column of smoke like those that went before Israel in the wilderness, and He would then bring the Jews back to the land. Many Jews and not a few Christians believed this teaching and, neglecting all else, spent much time in fasting, praying, doing penance, and performing good works.

Rabbi Joshua Ben-Levi had a dream, in which he saw the prophet Elijah at the entrance of Rabbi Simeon Ben-Yohai's cave. The rabbi asked Elijah, "When will the Messiah come?" Elijah replied that the rabbi could ask the Messiah Himself, for he could find the Messiah sitting among the beggars at the main gate of Rome. Rabbi Joshua Ben-Levi found the Messiah just where the prophet Elijah told him to look. In answer to his inquiry, the Messiah said that he would come, "Today!" On the following day, the rabbi met Elijah again and complained that the Messiah had spoken falsely to him, for he did not come on the day he said that he would. However, Elijah clarified the answer of the Messiah by explaining that he meant, "Today—if ye would but hearken to His voice!"

Rabbi Jacob was sure that during a certain year the Messiah would come. However, at the end of the year the Messiah's advent had not occurred. Rabbi Jacob then said to his favorite disciple, "The common people have repented and have turned from their evil ways. They are not the reason that the Messiah has not come. It is the scholars that bar the way for they are too proud to attain unto humility. The Messiah cannot come until the scholars become humble and repent!"

An Hasidic story recounts the time that Rabbi Menachem was visiting Palestine, and a foolish person climbed the Mount of Olives, and sounded a blast from a shofar. Rumor quickly spread through the terror-stricken populace that this was the trumpet blast announcing the day of the Messiah's advent. When the report reached Rabbi Menachem, he opened the windows and looking out upon the world, said, "I see no renewal there."

After the death of his beloved wife, a famous rabbi was heard to say, "You know, O Lord, that there is nothing in my power I would not have done to bring my wife back to life, if it were possible. Yet Thou, the All Powerful doth not restore Thy spouse Israel, though Thou are able to do so." And then the Lord answered, "Were Israelis as loyal to Me as your wife was to you, I would have long ago redeemed her!"

All of this indicates the rabbinic attitude toward the Messianic age. It is established by the Messiah, but it is posited upon Israel's own righteousness as a prerequisite to its establishment. Since the virtue of all Jews was necessary to the descent of the Messiah, it was incumbent upon each Jew to urge all other Jews to obey the law. The rabbis said, "Each Jew has within himself an element of the Messiah which he is required to purify and mature. Messiah will come when Israel has brought him to perfection of growth and purity within themselves."

However, in contrast to the Orthodox Jewish view of the regathering of Israel and the ushering in of the Messianic age, a biblical eschatology sees Israel regathered while they are as they were yesterday—yet in unbelief. This follows the sequence laid down by the prophets. Spiritual regeneration occurs only after Israel is back in the land. Israel's regeneration and the ushering in of the Messianic age occur simultaneously at the second coming of Christ. Israel is passive, except for her repentance at Messiah's advent. It is God who brings in the golden age of Messiah's reign when the Lord Jesus Christ returns to earth a second time.

3

ISRAEL'S MASADA COMPLEX

MASADA IS AN ANCIENT FORTRESS built by Herod the Great on the top of a mountain which rises above the floor of the wilderness of Judea. To the west of this mountain lies the Dead Sea, sluggish in the brilliant sunlight. Heat specters dance above its brackish surface, evaporating the water as fast as the river Jordan can feed it in. The sheer cliffs of Masada arise 1300 feet to a flat, windswept, plateau on its summit. This summit, which is shaped roughly like a ship, contains twenty-three acres, measuring some 1900 feet long and 650 feet wide. The prow of the ship points north.

Masada is a Hebrew word which comes to us through the Greek and means "Fortress." Masada is a rock. It stands sublime and unmovable in the midst of the Judean desert. Through the centuries earthquakes have shaken this massive monolith. The winter waters have swirled down the waddies and have slashed at its base to erode it. The Tenth Legion of Rome, aided by thousands of slaves, pounded away at it. With the exception of a few years during the Byzantine period when some monks occupied the site, this fortress has been uninhabited for the last two thousand years.

The rock of Masada is a symbol of the endurance of Israel. The monolithic unity of the nation Israel, which has remained distinctive and unique since the people were driven from the land in the aftermath of the Great Revolt, is like the rock of Masada. Israel's very survival as a people has been constantly threatened during the last two thousand years.

However, Israel stands today, people who have been dispersed among the nations for twenty centuries without interruption and yet have remained identifiable as Jews. They, too, arise out of the nations today as a distinct national monolith—even as the rock of Masada arises above the harsh landscape of the Judean wilderness.

However, the significance of Masada lies not in its physical features. In Masada, modern Israel has found a symbol of its own will—never again to endure servile existence, preferring death instead. Masada has personified Israel's determination not to be moved again from the land. This determination was dramatically portrayed in the events which took place on the summit of Masada in A.D. 73 when 960 Jewish men, women, and children, chose the dignity of death rather than live out their lives in abased submission to their Roman conquerors.

At one of the most strategic spots on the northern summit of Masada, close to the gate which leads to the water path, volunteer archaeological workers recently came across eleven pieces of broken pottery—ostraca. These were different from any other sherds found at Masada. On each was inscribed a different name in Hebrew. Apparently the same person had written these names on each of the fragments, for the handwriting was similar. The names were odd in that they seemed to be nicknames. Josephus records an event which took place during the final assault of Masada by the Romans and which may have involved these eleven pieces of broken pottery. He says, "They [the Jewish defenders of Masada] then chose ten men by lot out of them, to slay all the rest; everyone of whom laid himself down by his wife and children on the ground, and threw his arms about them, and they offered their necks to the stroke of those who by lot executed that melancholy office; and when these ten had, without fear, slain them all, they made the same rule for casting lots for themselves, that he whose lot it was should first kill the other nine, and after all, should kill himself."[1] Professor Yigael Yadin, who led the dig at Masada, believes that these eleven fragments, one of which contains the name Ben Ya'ir, are the very lots used to determine who should kill the remaining defenders of Masada. He contends that the plain inscription, Ben Ya'ir, used at that time on Masada, could have no other reference than to Eleazar Ben Ya'ir who was the Zealot commander of the fortress in its defense against the Romans.

It was this Eleazar Ben Ya'ir, his companions, and their heroic stand in which they chose death in preference to life under Roman slavery, that has been an inspiration to modern Israel's will to survive. Today Israel lives with the threat of military defeat and the moral degradation of national servitude again. It was the intrepid stand by the Jewish Zealots on Masada which ended the history of the Great Revolt. But by their choice of death rather than slavery, they elevated Masada to a symbol of Jewish resolution never again to fall prey to the nations. It is this national will to survive in the nobility of freedom which brings the new recruits for the armoured units of Israel's defense forces to the summit of Masada to take their oath of allegiance. There they affirm, "Masada shall never fall again!"

What happened on the windy heights of this mountain nearly two thousand years ago to cause it to become a national symbol of the Jews' determination to survive? What is this strange psychology which we call Israel's Masada complex?

When Titus had finished with the destruction of the city of Jerusalem and the demolition of the second temple, he returned to Rome in triumph. Thousands of Jewish slaves, along with the temple treasures, were taken to the Roman capital for the triumphant procession. The Great Revolt in Judea has been put down. However, Titus must have been haunted by the awareness that the Great Revolt had not really ended. For away down in the Judean desert, on the coast of the Dead Sea, atop a mountain, there was nearly a thousand Jewish Zealots who had not yet been subdued. In fact they were to hold out for three more years after the fall of Jerusalem. Titus dispatched General Flavius Silva, in command of the Tenth Roman Legion, to subdue Masada. From the heights of Masada, Eleazar and his Zealots could see the fierce Roman forces surrounding the base of the mountain. The Tenth Roman Legion was composed of five thousand or more foot soldiers, plus what may have amounted to several thousand more auxiliaries. Among these were a cavalry, bowmen, and slingmen. In addition, there was an artillery made up of great catapults, ballistas, and battering rams, which could level the most formidable of walls, as they had only recently leveled the walls of Jerusalem.

Access to Masada was by a narrow, winding, footpath called the Snake Path. It took approximately an hour for one to climb to the top of the mountain by this route. Josephus said that the path resembled a serpent "in its narrowness, and its perpetual windings."[2] Obviously General Silva could not take Masada in this way. Neither could he abide his time hoping to starve them out. Even though the country was very arid, the defenders had provisions enough for many months. Water was stored in great cisterns which had been built by King Herod. These filled annually with the winter rain. When the fortress finally fell, Eleazar gave orders that the remaining supply of food not be destroyed in order to impress the Romans that they were never wanting for food and water.

In response to the challenge, the Romans built a massive ramp up to the top of the mountain, using earth, stone, and wood. Since Silva's work force was composed of thousands of Jewish slaves recently captured in the Great Revolt, it was impossible for the defenders of Masada to rain down rocks and hot oil on these builders, lest they kill their own brothers. The ramp is 215 yards long and ended about 20 yards below the casement walls of Masada. It is still standing today and is one of the most remarkable examples of a Roman siege structure to be found anywhere in the world. Up this ramp General Silva's men and their Jewish slaves pushed the heavy siege equipment. Finally a great battering ram was brought up which would eventually break down this section of the wall of Masada, enabling the Roman soldiers to pour into the fortress with intent to pillage, rape, murder, and destroy all that was left within.

In the year A.D. 73, on the fifteenth of the month Nisan, 960 Jewish Zealots killed themselves rather than be taken into slavery by the Romans. It was the first day of the Passover. Josephus says, "Now for the Romans, they expected that they should be fought in the morning, when accordingly they put on their armour, and laid bridges of planks upon their ladders from their banks, to make an assault upon the fortress, which they did; but saw nobody as an enemy, but a terrible solitude on every side, with a fire within the place, as well as perfect silence. So they were at a loss to guess at what had happened. At length they made a shout, as if it had been at a blow given by a battering-ram, to try whether they could bring any one out that was within; the women* heard this noise and came out of their underground cavern and informed the Romans what had been done, as it was done; and the second of them clearly described all both what was said and what was done, and the manner of it; yet did they not easily give their attention to such a desperate undertaking, and did not believe it could be as they said; they also attempted to put the fire out, and quickly cutting themselves a way through it, they came within the palace, and so met with the multitude of the slain, but could take no pleasure in the fact, though it were done to their enemies. Nor could they do other than wonder at the courage of their resolution, and at the immovable contempt of death which so great a number of them had shown, when they went through with such an action as that was."[3]

And now, two thousand years later, modern Israel has determined that Masada shall not fall again! This Masada affirmation to remain a free people in their own land has been ratified by four wars which have engaged the Jews since they became an independent state in 1948. In each of these armed conflicts, against odds that seemed to be insurmountable, Israel came off victorious. And today, neither the hostility of the hoards of Arabs which surround her—and Israel is the only nation on earth completely surrounded by hostile and belligerent people, as was Masada—nor the threatening specter of the Soviet Union, nor the intimidations of the United Nations, nor the periodic reserve of the United States, has caused Israel to waver from this commitment. The land belongs to Israel. Her people will never again

---

*Two women on Masada failed to carry through Eleazar Ben Ya'ir's plan for mass suicide. They later related the events of the last hours of Masada. Josephus did not witness the fall of Masada as he had witnessed the fall of Jerusalem. Since he was, by the spring of A.D. 73, in Rome, the Roman soldiers must have relayed the account of the two women to him.

suffer the humiliation of physical and moral surfdom. Masada shall never fall again. This is the firm resolve, which we believe to be backed by a divine purpose for the nation Israel.

When Israel's Declaration of Independence had been signed by the delegates on that May afternoon in 1948 in the Tel Aviv Museum, at the close of the ceremonies two governmental officials picked up the parchment scroll and hurried down a steel staircase into an underground vault beneath the museum. There they placed the precious documents in a safe. If the Egyptian planes, which were even then on that *erev* Shabbat poised toward Tel Aviv, should level the city, the documents would be saved for posterity. Even if the new nation were destroyed, another generation of Jewish Zionists would try again. However, the new nation was not destroyed, even though four different Arab attempts would be made in the next twenty-five years to carry out the threat of total destruction for Israel. These attempts by the Arabs to destroy Israel are called by the Israelis: the War of Independence, 1948; the Sinai Campaign, 1956; the Six Day War, 1967; and the Yom Kippur War, 1973.

The first attempt came in the first few hours of the new state's existence. The initial invasion of Israel by her Arab neighbors began at the first glimmer of dawn on the first day after Israel had been reborn as a sovereign state. The armies of King Abdullah ibn-Husein were moving down a road toward the Jordan Valley. They came in tanks, armored cars, and trucks carrying soldiers. Crossing the Jordan at the Allenby Bridge, they moved toward the ancient oasis of Jericho. Other Arab legions were also on the move in Israel. In the south, Egyptian troops crossed into the sandy wastes of the Negev Desert and overran Jewish villages on the road to Gaza. Syrian and Lebanese troops attacked Jewish settlements in Galilee. These were the formal invasions during Israel's War of Independence. Actually the Arab-Israeli war had begun five and one-half months before, during the civil conflict which erupted when the United Nations declared the partition of Palestine, back in November, 1947. In the early days of this conflagration the Jews suffered the most. This was due to the pro-Arab attitude of the British, who were administering the last days of the mandate by restricting the flow of arms to the Jews and by suppressing the activity of the Hagana—the Jewish underground army.

At last, when the British withdrew at the end of the mandate, the new Israeli army—the *Tseva Hagana LeIsrael*, the Defense Army of Israel—could move unrestricted, and the tide soon turned. The Arab League was checked on every front. Fighting halted temporarily on June 11, 1948, as both sides accepted a United Nations truce. However, it resumed again on July 9, but was again halted by UN intervention ten days later. Clashes between Arabs and Jews erupted periodically thereafter until hostilities came to a final halt early in 1949.

The contending forces of the Arab legions—Egypt, Lebanon, Jordan, and Syria—signed an armistice agreement, and the new State of Israel was left with her original territory plus half as much again as was originally designated by the partition plan of the UN! It is interesting that each time the Arabs have contended with Israel over the territory which Israel already possesses, the Arabs lose more territory as a result of the contest. Newly captured territory included western Galilee, the city of Jaffa, the New City of Jerusalem, and a corridor from Jerusalem to the coast. The Arab state, which was proposed in the original UN partition plan for Palestine, was never realized, for Jordan seized the territory west of the Jordan river, along with the Old City of Jerusalem, and Egypt took the Gaza Strip.

How could the new State of Israel stand, and ultimately come out victorious, over many millions of belligerent Arabs who completely surrounded her? The most important reason was that the Jews had a will to win. They had a cause, a life-and-death situation. The Arabs did not. When defeat came after their first hours of victory, the Arabs became completely demoralized. Israel, in contrast, was determined that Masada shall not fall again!

However, apart from this all-important Masada complex—this intrinsic will to survive—Israel did have some outside help. They were not completely isolated. Even while the UN was debating the Palestine question, there were fifty-two Jewish training camps operating in Europe, in which officers and men were being prepared for the coming war in Palestine.

When the War of Independence started in 1948, Jewish volunteers poured into the Holy Land from Africa, Europe, and America. In fact, twenty percent of the Israeli army was composed of volunteers from outside the nation itself. In addition, American Jews poured vast sums of money into the new state. Golda Meir herself raised millions of dollars among American Jews at the outbreak of hostilities with the Arabs. Someone has defined a Zionist as "one Jew who takes money from another Jew to send a third Jew to the Holy Land." However, during the days of Israel's War of Independence, many gave as never before in order to keep the Jews in the Holy Land.

But the Israelis had not only a will to survive, they acted as if they intended to survive. There is an old Jewish saying that the reason Jacob put a stone under his head for a pillow was that he needed something to throw at the Arabs in case they attacked him. So the new state would forestall any illusions of a temporary occupation by immediately acting out their intention to protect themselves and to possess the land. The next day after the Sabbath, the first work day of the new State of Israel, immigrants began to flow in. Within three weeks every department of the new government had been set up and was in operation. Money was issued—printed in both Hebrew and Arabic. The supreme court was installed. During the summer a merchant marine was established. By the fall of 1948, El Al, the Israeli national airline, had begun operations. Before peace came the next summer, the first Knesset was elected, along with the first president of Israel, Chaim Weizmann. By that time things were judged stable enough to allow the United States Export-Import Bank to loan Israel a hundred million dollars. In May 1949, Israel became a member of the United Nations. What was to be the crowning act of the new state occurred on July 5, 1950, when the Law of Return was enacted. This confirmed the right of every Jew to dwell in Israel.

Between 1949 and 1953, Israel prospered. The goal of massive immigration and economic expansion was realized.

However, from 1953 until 1956 things worsened in the new nation. Egypt, who was being supplied with arms by the Russians, grew more aggressive. While Egypt grew stronger, the Western powers were reluctant to supply Israel with needed arms. Border incidents became an ever-increasing menace as the *fedayeen*, Arab raiders, moved deeper and deeper into Israeli territory from their bases in Sinai. In July 1956, Nasser nationalized the Suez Canal, and Israeli ships were barred from its facilities. Nasser encircled Israel with an Arab alliance which united Egypt, Jordan, and Syria in a unified Arab military command. Six days later, on October 29, 1956, Israel invaded Sinai and drove all the way to the Suez Canal. While undertaking the destruction of fedayeen bases in Sinai, Israel took six thousand Egyptian prisoners and vast quantities of supplies. Britain and France called for a cease-fire and a withdrawal by both sides from a ten-mile area around the Suez Canal. Israel agreed. Egypt refused. An Anglo-French invasion of Suez occurred on October 31, in which Port Said was bombed, and the allied French and British forces occupied the Suez area. In the UN resolution of November 7, 1956, supported by the United States and Russia, France and Britain were forced to withdraw. Israel withdrew also when she was given a guarantee that a United Nations Emergency Force would keep the peace and that Israel would be given free access to the Gulf of Akaba, which Egypt had previously blocked.

The decade between 1957 and 1967 was one in which Israel managed to live in relative peace with the Arabs. There were but a few border incidents. Israel's economy continued to grow. But most of all, Israel's military strength grew. David Ben-Gurion, the first prime minister of Israel, and his successor, Levi Eshkol, pursued a program of modernizing the armed forces. This was made possible to a large extent by an open supply of arms from France. In addition, by 1960 the world armament market had become a buyer's market, and arms flowed freely into Israel. The emphasis was upon air power and armor.

But things began to worsen in the Middle East as the Soviet Union became more and more active there. In February, 1966, a regime sympathetic to Russia came to power in Syria. In order to establish itself, the new Syrian government sponsored a renewal of border aggression against Israel. New raids were undertaken into Israeli territory. Jordan was implicated by the Syrians also. Israel retaliated with raids into Jordanian territory and with air raids on Syrian border positions. The Soviets, fearing that the regime in Syria might fall, instigated a mutual defense pact between Syria and Egypt in 1966. However, this failed to impress Israel. Finally, in May 1967, Russia persuaded Nasser, whose prestige was very low in his own country, to act in order to keep Israel from further retaliation against Syria.

On May 14, Nasser ordered his country to mobilize and began to gather troops on the border in Sinai in order to intimidate Israel. Nasser further ordered the UN troops out of his side of the border in Sinai and away from the Gulf of Akaba. Encouraged by a new popularity at home, on May 22, 1967, Nasser closed the Gulf of Akaba to Israeli shipping.

The situation became intolerable. The United States, busy with the war in Vietnam and threatened with student and racial anarchy at home, was unable to bring pressure to bear in order to relieve the situation. On June 5, 1967, Israel struck at her enemies and, in one of the most brilliant campaigns in the annals of war, completely defeated them in less than a week. In the first day of the war, Israel gained complete control of the air by virtually destroying the entire air force of Egypt, Jordan, and Syria. In rapid thrusts, Israeli troops then overran the entire Sinai Peninsula, including Sharm al-Sheikh, and drove to the eastern bank of the Suez Canal. The Gaza Strip was also taken, along with Jordanian-occupied Jerusalem. All the rest of Jordan's holdings on the west bank of the Jordan river were taken, including the major cities of Bethlehem, Hebron, Jericho, Nablus, Ramallah, and Jenin. From Galilee, Israeli forces drove into Syria until her armor stood before the gates of Damascus. Israel secured the Golan Heights, from which Israeli fishing on the Sea of Galilee and border villages had been shelled by the Syrians during nearly twenty years of Israel's existence.

Egypt suffered the most. Seven divisions totaling 80,000 to 100,000 men were completely routed or destroyed. The

entire armored force which Egypt had in Sinai, composed of
600 to 700 Soviet supplied tanks, was destroyed. More than
100 undamaged tanks fell into Israeli hands. Huge quantities
of Soviet-supplied equipment were taken from Egypt, including 400 field guns, 50 self-propelled guns, and literally
thousands of vehicles, along with large caches of ammuni-
tion and provisions of all kinds. Four hundred forty-four
Arab planes were destroyed on the ground when Israel
attacked airfields in Egypt, Jordan, Syria, and Iraq.

The major air thrust was against Egypt. Israeli planes, up
from fields near Tel Aviv and flying 150 feet above the
Mediterranean in order to avoid radar detection, swept into
Egypt from the sea and devastated Egyptian air bases from
Cairo to Suez and to the Red Sea coast. Soviet-supplied
MiG-21s and MiG-19s were lined up neatly in rows: all of
them were obliterated by Israeli jets. Sixteen Egyptian air
fields were put out of commission during the first hours of
the war. Twenty-six Egyptian radar screens were destroyed.
During the raids only two MiG-21s got off the ground and
they were soon shot down—but only after they had managed
to down two Israeli planes. It is believed that 100 out of
Egypt's 350 pilots were killed on the ground during this first
Israeli air strike.

Russia had supplied Egypt with several billion dollars'
worth of military equipment since 1955—most of which was
lost to Israel in a matter of hours. When the cease-fire came,
Israel had gained the Gaza Strip; the whole of the Sinai
Peninsula; all of Jordan's west bank territory, including the
Old City of Jerusalem; and the Golan Heights. The Arab
states had been delivered a crippling blow, and Soviet Russia received a major setback in the Middle East.

For the next six years the Arabs would gall under the
humiliating defeat of the Six-Day War. In addition to the loss
of Sinai, some territory on the West Bank, the Golan
Heights, and the Old City of Jerusalem, the Arabs had also
lost face. This must be recovered. Arab self-respect must be
regained as well as their conquered territory reclaimed. The
crushed ego of the Arab again surfaced as new hostility
broke out during Israel's twenty-fifth anniversary year. In
October 1973, on the Day of Atonement, the Arabs again

invaded Israeli-held territory. The fourth war Israel was to fight with the Arabs began on October 6 and is called the Yom Kippur War. It lasted for eighteen days. This time Israel lost some territory, and the Arabs regained some self respect.

The fighting concentrated in the south on the borders of Egypt along the Suez Canal. In the north, fighting erupted on the Golan Heights, where Israel faced the troops of Syria who were joined a few days later by troops from Jordan and from Saudi Arabia. The Israeli forces experienced some initial setback from the Russian-equipped army of Egypt which occupied territory east of the Suez Canal. However, in the north, Israel began to drive toward Damascus. Soon Israeli troops were also to invade Egypt. When the United Nations finally was able to enforce a cease-fire, the Israeli troops were within twenty miles of Damascus. They had also established a bridgehead into Egypt, where they occupied territory on the west bank of the Suez Canal extending from Ismailia in the north down to Adabiya. Suez City was taken by Israeli troops. But to counterbalance this territorial acquisition, the Egyptian 2d and 3rd corps occupied an area in Sinai east of the canal. When the war ended, these Egyptian troops found themselves cut off and surrounded by hostile forces. Only United Nations intervention succeeded in getting a relief column to them in order to supply food and water to these Egyptian troops captured in the desert.

The war in the Middle East became a major threat to world peace when Russia declared her intentions to send troops unilaterally into the area to guarantee no more Israeli aggression. On October 25, President Nixon placed the United States military forces on a worldwide military alert. Finally the United Nations succeeded in sending to the Middle East a peacekeeping force composed of troops from a number of other countries, and the threat of world war subsided for the moment. Israel agreed to withdraw several miles back into the Sinai desert, there to await the Geneva peace talks.

U.S. News and World Report, in its predictions for 1974, said,

Western diplomats say that despite Syria's boycott of the talks at Geneva—due to reopen later in January—there is hope of an eventual settlement. As never before, these experts say, the U.S. is throwing its weight behind negotiations for peace. Moreover, Russia—after exploiting the conflict for more than 15 years—now seems to have decided it stands to gain from reducing Mideast tensions, at least for the present. This optimism is not shared by the Arab nations or by Israel. Many Israelis remain convinced the Arabs are irrevocably dedicated to ultimate destruction of the Jewish state. The Arabs doubt that the U.S. can force Israel to return all Arab territory seized in the 1967 war or to compromise on the stickiest question of all—control of Arab Jerusalem, the holy city, and finding a home for displaced Palestinians.[4]

Israel's Masada complex has served well as a mighty incentive to sustain her in the face of monumental obstacles. These problems which modern Israel—the Third Commonwealth—faced during the first years of her existence were not unlike the problems faced by Israel's Second Commonwealth, which was established when Israel returned from the Babylonian captivity in the sixth century B.C. In fact, there are three parallels which should be noted.

The first parallel between the two communities, separated now by twenty-five hundred years, is that both the Second Commonwealth (Israel after the Babylonian captivity) and the Third Commonwealth (modern Israel) were created by an outside power. Israel's Second Commonwealth was created by the edict of Cyrus the Great, king of Persia, in 537 B.C. It is recorded in Ezra 1:1-4.

Modern Israel—her Third Commonwealth—was created by the United Nations Partition Plan which passed the General Assembly on November 29, 1947, by a vote of 33 to 13. This was the plan recommended by the eleven-member United Nations Special Committee on Palestine, set up to investigate the British request that the mandate be ended. Israel's Second Commonwealth had fallen when Titus took the city of Jerusalem in A.D. 70. When the UN Partition Plan for Palestine was passed in Flushing Meadows, New York, the Jews in Rome remembered Titus. Almost instinctively the Jews gathered at the Arch of Titus, which had been set up in the ancient Forum to commemorate the fall of the Judean state. Cheering, singing, and weeping, several thousand Jews—contrary to Orthodox practice—marched under and around the Arch of Titus to celebrate the return to the land after nearly two thousand years of exile.

The second parallel between ancient Israel after the Babylonian exile and modern Israel is that both had internal conflicts between the secular and religious. In modern Israel there is a militant group of Jews called the *Naturei Karta* which will not accept the present state at all. They represent most dramatically the conflict within modern Israel between the secular and the religious. To them, Israel's Independence Day is a day of mourning. Unlike the Jewish Zealots of the first century whose wrath was directed against Rome, these modern day zealots have turned their wrath against fellow Jews who support the present State of Israel. This group of orthodox Jewish zealots live largely in the *Mea-Shearim* section of Jerusalem. They believe that *HaKodesh Baruch Hu* (the Holy One, blessed be He) will establish the sovereign State of Israel when Messiah comes. The present "blasphemous state" is premature, for the Jews must suffer under foreign rule until Messiah's advent. The Naturei Karta thrives in a crowded section of Jerusalem filled with small synagogues, ritual baths, and houses of Torah study.

Their mode of life is remindful of that which their ancestors knew in Eastern Europe. The men of this Hasidic sect, which dominates the section, dress in seventeenth century garb; they are bearded figures in long black caftan topcoats with side curls flapping against their ears. During the week, their heads are always covered with a hat, a *yarmulke*, which is a skullcap. On the Sabbath they wear robes of silk and hats trimmed with fur. The women of Mea-Shearim follow the orthodox code of law and are clothed in long dresses of print material. Their heads are shaven and are covered with wigs or with scarves. In the Mea-Shearim quarter of Jerusalem, picture taking is forbidden—"thou shalt not make graven images."

Ancient observances are imposed upon all with meticulous care. Signs warn, "Our Torah requires Jewish women to be attired in modest dress, sleeves reaching below the elbows [slacks are forbidden], stockings; married women have their head covered. These are the virtues of Jewish women throughout the ages." All roads leading into this section of Jerusalem are barricaded on Sabbath eve. To violate one of their traditions is to risk being stoned. Even a noisy or flamboyantly dressed pedestrian is blocked from entering. However, they have not confined their Sabbath observance to their own section. On occasions they have gone out into the city to forcibly protest the movement of traffic, sporting events, and the use of swimming pools by both men and women. And they do not hesitate to rock public transportation if it moves on the Sabbath. Quite often police must break up a Saturday afternoon fight between nonobservant, T-shirted, Jerusalem youths and Hasidic youths in fur-brimmed Sabbath hats who have ventured out of Mea-Shearim to throw stones at Sabbath violators.

Not all orthodox Jews are Naturei Karta, but twenty five thousand of them in Jerusalem are attempting to lead the lives that their forefathers lived three hundred years ago in the ghettos of Eastern Europe. They are the Jews who separate themselves from the mainstream of Jewish life by their fundamentalist attitude toward the existence of the State of Israel itself. They abhor the blasphemous presumption of those Jews who, with Gentile help, have assumed the prerogative of the Messiah in establishing the new State of Israel. In fact, they believe that the State will yet suffer destruction because of this presumption upon the divine prerogatives of the Messiah. Therefore, they fast, they refuse to pay taxes, they utterly reject the government of Israel, they refuse to register for military service. So strong are their feelings that they will not even pray at the Western Wall since its liberation during the Six-Day War. It is they who constantly agitate against the performing of autopsies and harass the pathologists among the Israeli medical profession. They believe that transgressions of the law, such as this, along with the profaning of the Sabbath are examples of the sins of the people which are delaying the coming of the Messiah.

However, though there is today, in Israel's Third Commonwealth, this internal conflict between the secular and the religious, this struggle is not new. It occurred early in the Second Commonwealth immediately after the return from Babylonian exile in the fifth and sixth centuries B.C. Two groups were then in opposition to each other ideologically. One group was represented by Zerubbabel, grandson of King Jehoiachin, who would have established a secular authority vested in the house of David. Joshua, grandson of the high priest Seriah, maintained that the leadership of the new community should have a religious basis and should rest in the priestly family. The divine choice of Zerubbabel may be reflected in Haggai 2:23: "In that day, saith the LORD of hosts, will I take thee, O Zerubbabel, my servant, the son of Shealtiel, saith the LORD, and will make thee as a signet; for I have chosen thee, saith the LORD of hosts."

The third similarity between ancient Israel after the Babylonian exile and modern Israel after 1948 is that both were greatly resented by their neighbors. It was the Samaritans who resented the Second Commonwealth and did everything possible to subvert its successful establishment. The Samaritans, who were the descendants of the Assyrian colony planted by Shalmaneser after the fall of the Northern Kingdom of Israel, constantly harassed the returning exiles of Judah. These Judeans had been gone for seventy years or more. The land now was claimed by those who had been there for those many years while Judah was away in Babylonian exile.

But just as the returning exiles were resented by the inhabitants of the land in the sixth century B.C., so the inhabitants of the land resented the returning Jewish exiles in the twentieth century A.D. The Arabs feel that their claim to the land is far more viable than that of the Jews.

Arab claim to the land of Palestine was based largely on two things. First, they had been present in the land since the first Muslim caliph ruled in the seventh century A.D. However, contrary to popular opinion, the land was not held exclusively by Arabs during all these years. There have always been Jews in what is today the State of Israel.[5] Second, the Arab claim to Palestine was based on a secret agreement which was contained in correspondence written in 1915 between Sir Henry McMahon, British High Commissioner in Egypt, and Sherif Husein of Mecca. In return for Arab assistance against the Turks in World War I, the British would "recognize and support independence of the Arab regions [formally belonging to the Ottoman Turkish Empire] within the limits demanded by the Sherif of Mecca." This comprised a million square miles of Arab territory to be taken from the Turks and, as the Arabs understood it, included Palestine. Later, in 1922, Winston Churchill insisted that it was never the intention of Britain to include Palestine in the 1915 pledge to the Arabs. At this time he also reaffirmed Britain's adherence to the Balfour Declaration.

Arab animosity toward the new State of Israel was seen from the very first. When the United Nations voted yes on the Partition Plan for Palestine, the Arab delegations from Iraq, Syria, Lebanon, Egypt, Saudi Arabia, and Yemen arose and walked out in protest. The Arabs predicted the death of the United Nations Charter as a result of this move in Palestine. All Arab delegations announced that they would boycott the partition plan and have nothing further to do with the UN discussions on Palestine. *Time* magazine for that week predicted that the name of the new state would be New Judea, but the Arabs were declaring there would be no new state to name. The Council of *Ulema* (sages) of Cairo's Al-Azhar University—the spiritual leadership of present-day Islam—formally proclaimed a holy war against the Jews.

Abraham traversed the Fertile Crescent, originally coming from Ur of the Chaldees (Babylon) in southwest Mesopotamia. He migrated to Haran, northwest of Ur. Subsequently he came by way of Canaan to Egypt. These two empires, Egypt and Babylon, represent the two termini of the Fertile Crescent. God gave all the land between them to Abraham and to his seed, saying, "Unto thy seed have I given this land, from the river of Egypt unto the great river, the river Euphrates" (Gen 15:18). During the reign of Solomon, Israel possessed more of this original territory than ever before. However, Israel never has possessed all the territory that God promised Abraham and his descendants. Today, as a result of the conquests of the Six-Day War, Israel does occupy territory almost to the borders of Egypt. But northward their occupation stops on the Golan Heights.

The Fertile Crescent, which now belongs to Syria and Iraq, has never been occupied by Israel. But this was originally a part of the land granted to Abraham and his descendants which makes up the Fertile Crescent between Egypt and Babylon. When God gave this territory to Abraham and his seed, He granted them a viaduct between these two great powers, over which the nations were to contend from the time of Abraham until the end of the great Tribulation period and the Battle of Armageddon. Its very location caused problems, because the land which Israel was to possess was actually a land bridge which connected three continents— Africa, Europe, and Asia. Since it was bounded on the west by the Mediterranean sea, and on the east by the Arabian desert, these few miles that lay between the sea and the desert were the only viable land link between the three continents. So strategic was this narrow land bridge which connected Egypt on the south and Babylon on the north, around the Fertile Crescent, that only God could keep it intact for Israel. When He did not, it was taken.

But what is Israel's claim to this land today? When the late prime minister David Ben-Gurion addressed the Jerusalem Conference on Biblical Prophecy, held in the city of Jerusalem in June 1971, he disavowed any Jewish claim to the land on strictly biblical grounds. Sensing that those in attendance at the conference were sympathetic with Israel's territorial claims, but from a biblically oriented standpoint, Ben-Gurion maintained that the Jews had a territorial right simply as a people. They are a national entity. Therefore, they are entitled to a national home as is any other national group. This is their due in the very nature of things, and not because of any unique relationship to *Yahweh*, the covenant God of Israel.

When Herzl wrote *The Jewish State*, he considered the idea of a national home for the Jews in Argentina. The Zionist leaders also gave careful consideration to Britain's

1903 offer of territory in Uganda. If Jewish right to a national home was based solely upon the fact that any nation is due a place to exist, then any place suitable would do. However, there is woven into the very soul of the Jew a desire to return, not to just any land for national settlement, but to *the* land. This suggests something more than a pragmatic argument for a Jewish national home. It suggests that there is a divine destiny for the Jew in which this relationship between him and Eretz Israel—the land of Israel—plays an important part. This homing instinct has brought the Jew back to the land. His Masada instinct will keep him there. Though the latter may have been learned from bitter experience, the former is innate and God-given.

Biblically, Israel's claim to the land rests upon the fact that God has made certain promises to the nation which are bound up in a covenant relationship. This covenant relationship is still valid after four thousand years. The covenant has four parts. They are sometimes called the Abrahamic covenant (Gen 12:1-3), the Palestinian covenant (Deu 30:1-8), the Davidic covenant (2 Sa 7:12-16) and the new covenant (Jer 31:31-34). The first two parts of the covenant relationship between God and the nation Israel we will examine here, for they contain Israel's title deed to the Holy Land. The remaining two parts of the covenant we will note in chapter five when Israel's coming golden age is discussed.

When God called Abram out of Ur of the Chaldees, He said, "Get thee out of thy country, and from thy kindred, and from thy father's house, unto the land that I will show thee: and I will make of thee a great nation, and I will bless thee, and make thy name great; and be thou a blessing: and I will bless them that bless thee, and him that curseth thee will I curse: and in thee shall all the families of the earth be blessed" (Gen 12:1-3). This basic covenant between God and Abraham, which also extends to his seed, is restated and reconfirmed, as well as enlarged, in Genesis 12:6-7; 13:14-17; 15:1-21; 17:1-14; and 22:15-18.

The promises which God made to Abraham were to benefit him personally. However, the great impact of the covenant's provisions have to do with Abraham's offspring. While some of Abraham's descendants—the seed of Ishmael (Gen 17:19-21), and those of Keturah (25:1-5), and those of his concubines (25:6)—are excluded from the covenant privileges, the physical descendants of Abraham, Isaac, and Jacob are heirs of the promises of the covenant.

Some promised blessings for Abraham's seed are these: They would become a great nation(12:2); they would be innumerable (13:16; 15:5); and in his seed all the nations of the earth will be blessed (12:3; 22:18; cf. Gal 3:8). In addition, they would be heirs of the land. This part of the covenant which gives Abraham's seed title deed to the land is stated in several different ways within the various reaffirmations of the covenant. "And the LORD appeared unto Abram, and said, Unto thy seed will I give this land" (12:7). "For all the land which thou seest, to thee will I give it, and to thy seed forever" (13:15). "In that day the LORD made a covenant with Abram, saying, Unto thy seed have I given this land, from the river of Egypt unto the great river, the river Euphrates" (15:18). "And I will give unto thee, and to thy seed after thee, the land of thy sojournings, all the land of Canaan, for an everlasting possession" (17:8). Therefore, an inseparable part of the Abrahamic covenant is the land which the seed are to possess.

The general provisions of the covenant made with Abraham have never been annulled. In addition, the specific provision of the covenant which concerns Israel's possession of the land is as valid today as it was when the covenant was first made. There are several principles that must be applied to the covenant made with Abraham when the contemporary validity of these provisions is evaluated. Is the ancient covenant which God made with Abraham and his seed as valid today as it was four thousand years ago? In answering this vital question, three things must be kept in mind.

First, the covenant and its provisions must be taken *literally* and not spiritually. There is a tendency to spiritualize the provisions of the covenant, thereby relieving them of any further significance for the nation Israel. This tendency rejects the idea that these covenant provisions are still valid today, maintaining instead that the nation Israel lost claim to these blessings when she rejected the Lord Jesus Christ as

Messiah. Instead of expecting a literal fulfillment of the covenant promises in the nation Israel, one is to see these promises as spiritually fulfilled in the church—"spiritual Israel." When a Jew reads this interpretation, he is quick to observe that though the positive blessings of the covenant are spiritualized and reapplied to the church, the curses are still applied literally to Israel in her rejection of the Lord Jesus Christ. It is sufficient for our purpose here to observe that all of the covenant provisions which have been fulfilled have been fulfilled literally. If the foregoing promises have all been literally fulfilled, and they have, then we should expect the remainder of them to be fulfilled just as literally. In fact, that is just what we are witnessing today—the literal return of the Jews back to the land just as the prophets predicted!

Second, the covenant and its provisions must be taken *prophetically* as well as historically. What has not been fulfilled is prophetic of what is to come for the nation Israel.

The events of the last fifty years which have restored Israel to the land again are providential and are in partial fulfillment of the covenant promises made to Abraham nearly four thousand years ago. We are seeing the literal fulfillment of the covenant promises today. Therefore, this dual confirmation composed of scriptural promise and contemporary historical fulfillment lends validity to the expectation that all the covenant promises will yet be literally fulfilled. These covenant promises contain not only reference to the seed of Abraham inheriting the land, but also provisions for the reign of the greater Son of David, the Lord Jesus Christ, Israel's Messiah, upon the throne of Israel during a golden age which is yet to come.

Third, the covenant and its provisions must be taken *unconditionally*. The fulfillment of the covenant provisions was not based on Israel's faithfulness, but on the unconditional promises of God. Because the covenant is unconditional, God used such terms as "eternal" and "everlasting" when it was given or reaffirmed. "And I will establish my covenant between me and thee and thy seed after thee throughout their generations for an everlasting covenant, to be a God unto thee and to thy seed after thee" (Gen 17:7).

"And my covenant shall be in your flesh for an everlasting covenant" (v. 13). "And I will establish my covenant with him for an everlasting covenant for his seed after him" (v. 19). "Remember his covenant for ever, The word which he commanded to a thousand generations, The covenant which he made with Abraham, And his oath unto Isaac, And confirmed the same unto Jacob for a statute, To Israel for an everlasting covenant, Saying, Unto thee will I give the land of Canaan" (1 Ch 16:15-18; cf. Ps 105:9-10).

In the covenant made with Abraham, God promised that the seed of Abraham would possess the land forever. Why, then, were the people of Israel dispossessed of the land on numerous occasions? The answer is that, within the framework of the unconditional covenant, exile, which was God's stipulated punishment for sin, could occur at any time as a result of Israel's sin (Deu 28:58-64). The covenant was not annulled as a result of Israel's sin, but exile could come as a result of it. Because of the sin of idolatry, Judah was exiled into Babylon in 587 B.C. (Jer 25:1-11). Because of their rejection of the Lord Jesus Christ as Messiah, Israel was again dispersed from the land, A.D. 135 until 1948 (Mt 23:37-39). But if Israel was exiled in unbelief, why is she being regathered today—still in unbelief? The prophetic Word indicates that Israel will receive the Lord Jesus Christ as Messiah (Mt 23:39), but Israel's Messianic experience must be in association with the land (Jer 23:5-8). This idea will be given further attention when we discuss the new covenant and the golden age in chapter five.

When the Israeli armed forces finally broke through the Jordanian defenses in the Old City of Jerusalem during the Six-Day War, the Western Wall lay open before them. The chief rabbi of the armed forces, General Shlomo Goren, stood before the Wall, clutching a Torah he had carried into the fallen city. A *Newsweek* reporter asked him if the Jewish people would ever again relinquish the city. He replied, "We took an oath today, while capturing the city—on our blood we took an oath—that we will never give it up. We will never leave this place. The Western Wall belongs to us. The holy places were ours first. From here we do not move. Never! Never!"

And so Israel has come back to Zion after two thousand years. The exile is over. They are again in possession of the land—by United Nations decree, and by right of victory when a belligerent neighbor attacked them. But most of all, the land is theirs because four thousand years ago Yahweh, the covenant God of Israel, elected them to His eternal purposes and made the possession of the land a part of that purpose. One day Israel's Messiah, the Lord Jesus Christ, will return, and they will receive Him as Messiah when they shall look upon Him whom they have pierced; and they shall mourn for Him (Zec 12:10). But until that day Israel will not be moved from off the land.

Masada shall not fall again!

4

THE BIRTH PANGS OF THE MESSIAH

AFTER THE NAZIS had murdered three hundred thousand Jews from the Warsaw ghetto, Alexander Donat wrote, "Above all we kept asking ourselves the age old question: why? why? What was all the suffering for? What had we done to deserve this hurricane of evil, this avalanche of cruelty? Why had all the gates of hell opened and spewed forth on us the furies of human vileness? What crime had we committed for which this might have been calamitous punishment? Where, in what code of morals, human or divine, is there a crime so appalling that innocent women and children must expiate it with their lives in martyrdom no torquemada ever dreamed of?"[1]

But no answer came—save the unalterable awareness that somehow the suffering of the Jew has an inexplicable part in human history and the assurance that God's providential care is woven throughout the fabric of Jewish agony.

It is little wonder that for centuries Jewish expositors have seen the nation Israel itself as the suffering servant in the prophet Isaiah's four great poems (42:1-4; 49:1-6; 50:4-11; 52:13—53:12). The unjustified and enigmatic suffering of the Jew is somehow bound up with the good of mankind, they believe. When Rabbi Yishmael's turn came to be tortured by his captors, the Romans, he heard a heavenly voice saying, "Yishmael, my son, keep quiet. If you weep, I shall throw the world back into chaos. One single tear will engulf all of creation." And Rabbi Yishmael did not weep. Some Jewish pietists, like the Hasidim, even hold to a tradition that there are thirty-six just men in each generation upon whose righteousness and suffering the world reposes. And, like Rabbi Yishmael, they must bear the reproaches of all mankind lest the world be thrown back into chaos. This myth is based on a Talmudic statement to the effect that there are in the world no fewer than thirty-six righteous men who greet the *Shekinah*—the divine Presence.² Isaiah 30:18 is also supposed to be an allusion to this group which is called the *Lamed-Vav*—the Hebrew term for thirty-six. This verse ends, "blessed are all they that wait for him." The Hebrew word translated "for him" has the numerical value of thirty-six. If it were not for these thirty-six men and their just lives, though they are indistinguishable from ordinary mortals and sometimes do not know themselves that they are of the Lamed-Vav, the world would suffocate in its own agony of suffering. It is they who suffer vicariously for all mankind as they assimilate in themselves the griefs of the world. When an unknown Lamed-Vav rises to heaven, so an Hasidic story goes, he is so frozen with agony that God must warm him a thousand years between His fingers before his soul can open itself to paradise. Some are so filled with human woe that God Himself cannot revive them. So from time to time the Creator, blessed be His name, sets forward the clock of the last judgment by one minute.

The history of the Jew has been a history of suffering. However, during the twentieth century, European Jewish people have endured suffering and persecution which even the horrors and the aftermath of the Great Revolt cannot rival. This epoch of intense agony for the Jews, called the Holocaust, will be superseded in history only by the great tribulation period when the suffering of the Jew will be "such as hath not been from the beginning of the world until now, no, nor ever shall be," (Mt 24:21). Perhaps the Holocaust has already preconditioned the world to accept the horror of the great tribulation period.

World War I had left Germany crushed. A scapegoat was needed upon whom the blame for the defeat of Germany could be placed. That scapegoat was found among less than one percent of the German people—the Jews. Hitler blamed them for the war and for all the ills that postwar Germany had fallen into. This anti-Semitic appeal drew support for Hitler from many quarters and enabled him to overthrow the Weimar republic, which was equated with Jewishness.

Though the German Jews were but one percent of the population, they had made vital contributions to German culture. They were fully assimilated, they believed. They were to learn differently. When Hitler came to power as chancellor of Germany in January 1933, one of his first acts was to issue an order for a one-day boycott of all Jewish shops. Mild as this now seems, this began the overt persecution of the Jews which was to come to an end twelve years later, after six million Jewish people had been insulted, beaten, robbed, starved, worked, raped, tortured, and finally murdered. At the close of World War II the Nuremberg trials (November 1945) revealed that there had been 5,721,800 Jewish victims of the Nazi Holocaust. The official indictment reads: "Of the 9,600,000 Jews who lived in the parts of Europe under Nazi domination, it is conservatively estimated that 5,700,000 have disappeared, most of them deliberately put to death by the Nazi conspirators."[3] Thus the round figure of six million is the generally accepted total for those who were exterminated during the Holocaust.

During the Third Reich, there were literally thousands of prisoners confined in prison camps, transit camps, and labor camps in Germany and the countries which the Nazis had occupied. The Jews were kept for a while in one or the other of these camps in order to extract from them the last ounce of physical effort. Later, exhausted, ill, starved, and maimed, they were sent to the death camps where Jews perished by the millions.

Persecution of the Jews began in Nazi Germany long before the war was to afford the final solution to the Jewish problem. These prewar persecutions of the Jew took two forms. First, there were the official acts which were to deprive the Jews of all human rights. The purpose was expressed in the German word, *Judenrein*—to rid Germany of the Jew. Officially, this studied exclusion of the Jew from Germany was set out in the Nuremberg Laws, which were passed in 1935. Among them were the Reich Citizenship

Laws, which distinguished between the subject of the state and a citizen of the Third Reich. A citizen was defined as one who was of German or cognate blood, thereby denying citizenship to German Jews. The Law for the Protection of the German Blood and German Honor forbade marriage or cohabitation between Jews and Germans. When these anti-Jewish laws were finally issued in their expanded form, they deprived the Jews not only of citizenship and the right to marry non-Jews, but by 1939, public schools were forbidden to Jewish children. The Jews could participate in practically no business, and the professions were denied to them. They could own no land. They could not associate with non-Jews. Public parks, libraries, and museums were closed to them. They were ordered to live in ghettos; and by 1941, they were forbidden the use of public transportation and public telephones. Jewish boys over twelve years of age were conscripted for work in the munitions factories, and all Jews over six years of age were to wear a yellow badge.

But there were also unofficial, though officially sanctioned, persecutions of the Jews in those days just before World War II. On the night of November 9, 1938, simultaneous riots against the Jews broke out all over Germany. These riots had been carefully prearranged by the Gestapo. The occasion was the murder of a third secretary in the German embassy in Paris. The murderer happened to be a Jew. This provided the excuse for a government-directed pogrom against the Jews. Gestapo Chief Reinhard Heydrich gave the orders: "Because of the attempt on the life of the Embassy Secretary vom Rath in Paris, demonstrations against the Jews are to be expected tonight, November 9th and 10th throughout the Reich." His orders went on to explain that the destruction of German property was to be avoided. Jewish flats and shops may be destroyed, but not looted. Synagogues may be burned if their demolition will not endanger adjacent property. Finally twenty thousand to thirty thousand Jews were to be arrested. Synagogue archives were to be turned over to the Gestapo.

On November 11, Hermann Goering received a report. Practically every synagogue in Germany had been destroyed. One hundred seventy-one apartment houses had been set on fire. Eight hundred fifteen shops had been looted. (The figure was later revised upward to 7,500.) Twenty-six Jews had been killed and thirty-six others badly wounded. Twenty thousand Jews had been arrested, and over half of them were sent to the concentration camps at Buchenwald. As a result of this night of rioting, the helpless Jews had their property confiscated. In addition, the Jewish community was fined a thousand million marks, and all damaged property was to be paid for by the Jews themselves without the benefit of insurance.

After losing their property, most of the German Jews were herded into ghettos or sent to concentration camps. Ultimately they were to be deported under the most inhuman conditions to Poland, where Hitler had determined that the final solution to the Jewish problem was to take place. Many Jews were shot. Others were merely starved and worked to death. Many died in forced marches. But in the end this was too slow and too expensive. Finally, mass extermination was attempted by the gas chambers of Auschwitz, Majdanek, Treblinka, Dachau, Buchenwald, Bergen-Belsen, and other death camps. After life was destroyed by poisonous gas, millions of Jewish bodies were destroyed in adjacent crematoriums. Many Jews whose will to resist had been sapped by years of indignity, persecution, and later by starvation, disease, and exhaustion, were herded into the gas chambers, not knowing until the last minute that this was their fate.

Adolph Hitler believed that the Jews were members of an inveterately evil race whose ultimate aim it was to destroy the superior Aryan race and to dominate the world. He also theorized the danger of "sexual contamination" by the Jews. Hitler even identified the Jew with a microbial infection. This led to the ultimate solution to the Jewish problem —extermination. The process began when the war put several million Jews in Eastern Europe at his disposal and at the same time released him from any moral necessity to justify his actions to the rest of the world. On July 31, 1941, Hermann Goering gave the order "to proceed with all the preparations necessary for organizing the complete solution to the Jewish question in the German sphere of influence in

Europe."⁴ The order was to be carried out by mass executions, annihilation by forced labor, disease in the ghettos and the concentration camps, and finally death by gas or shooting in the extermination camps. Hitler believed that in exterminating the Jewish "plague," he was rendering to humanity a service which his contemporaries could not imagine.

There are three characteristics of Hitler's treatment of the Jews during the Holocaust which indicates his pathological hatred of them as a race. First, his aim was to destroy Jews as Jews. Therefore, the Jewish victims of the Nazi included women, children, and old people. Second, the Jews were to be eradicated immediately, even while the war was in progress, while the fate of other peoples could be left to the end of the war to determine. There was a dread urgency about his dealing with the Jew. Third, Hitler's war with the Jews took priority over every other consideration. No other exigency was to take precedence over Hitler's design for the annihilation of the Jews. Even when railroad transportation facilities were desperately needed to transport troops and supplies to the front, priority was given by Himmler and Eichmann to the deportation of the Jews on these trains.

"In the end, as in the beginning, Hitler reviled the Jews. They were, he repeated, the cause of the war and the 'universal poisoner of all nations.' For the last time he charged the German people to 'uphold the law of race.' There was no word of remorse or regret for the ruined world he had made," observes Nora Levin.⁵ His hatred of the Jew would not leave him even in the frustration of defeat and the agony of death. As his body was consumed in flames, so his spirit was consumed in the canker of anti-Semitism.

Are we to see more in this man than just a defeated tyrant who articulated, and then implemented, a particularly virulent type of anti-Semitism? Were his aspirations for Nordic superiority at the cost of the annihilation of an entire nationality of people and his designs for personal aggrandizement merely the apparitions of a madman consumed with a pathological hatred for the Jews? Or was he the precurser of an even more sinister figure who will soon follow upon the stage of world history to reap an even greater horror upon the Jews? Israel Knox in the introduction to his, *Anthology of Holocaust Literature*, says,

> The animosity of the Nazis for the Jews was irrational and pathological, and the resolve to bring about total liquidation by means of a carefully planned process of genocide was at once so shrewd and so diabolical that only such as were equally demonic could envisage it and anticipate it, least of all the Jews, who, though the victims of persecution throughout two millennia, were not practitioners of it . . . . In Milton's, *Paradise Lost*, Lucifer avers: "Evil, be thou my god!" When evil is no longer just a deviation from the good, a heresy within the sphere of good, but is itself enthroned as the good, then the moral universe has been turned upside down and the sovereignty of Satan has been established. The Holocaust Kingdom was a Kingdom of Satan and those who served him. Isaiah's exhortation: "woe unto them who call evil good, and good evil," was exchanged for Lucifer's challenge: "Evil, be thou my god"—and the logic of the Holocaust was now crystal clear: it was the logic of a party, a country, a people that proclaimed Lucifer, in the guise of Hitler, to be King and decided to call evil good and to conduct themselves accordingly.[6]

This is a Jew writing. With no discernible appreciation for what the New Testament teaches about the coming Antichrist, this Jewish anthologist of the holocaust, in describing Nazi Germany under the rule of Hitler, also described the kingdom of the Antichrist and his attitude toward the Jews of the great tribulation period.

It is interesting that the idea of a great time of trouble for Israel—a holocaust—which will immediately precede the second coming of Christ is taught not only in the Bible; the idea also appears in other Jewish literature and is a vital part of the Orthodox Jewish Messianic expectation. Even before the first century, the idea of a pre-Messianic holocaust appears in the pseudepigrapha.[7] However, it is in the Talmud that we find the most numerous references to this idea, under the figure of "the birth pangs of the Messiah."

After the failure of the Bar Kokhba revolt and the severe persecutions of Hadrian which followed, many of the rabbis interpreted these to be the birth pangs of the true Messiah. They believed that the advent of the Messiah would be preceded by a time of intense woes for the Jews. Some of Rabbi Akiba's disciples who survived the aftermath of the fall of Bethar wrote of this time of Messianic travail.

Rabbi Nehemiah said, "In the generation when the son of David comes, impudence will increase and esteem will be perverted; the vine will yield its fruit but the wine will be costly; and the whole empire will be converted to heresy, with none to offer rebuke" (Sanhedrin 97a; Midrash R., Song of Songs 2.13).

Rabbi Judah said, "In the generation when the son of David comes, the meeting-place of scholars will be given over to harlotry. Galilee will be laid waste and Gablan be made desolate; and the people of the frontier will go about from city to city with none to take pity on them. The wisdom of the Scribes will become foolish, and they that shun sin will be despised. The face of this generation is as the face of a dog, and truth is lacking, as it is written: 'And truth shall be lacking, and he that departeth from evil maketh himself a prey'" (Sanhedrin 97a).

Rabbi Nehorai commented, "In the generation when the son of David comes, the young will insult their elders and the elders will wait upon the young; 'the daughter riseth up against her mother, the daughter-in-law against her mother-in-law;' and the face of this generation is as the face of a dog, and the son does not feel ashamed before his father" (Sanhedrin 97a; Pesikta Rabbati 15.15).

Rabbi Simeon Ben Yohai predicted, "In the week* when the son of David comes, in the first year this verse will be fulfilled: 'I will cause it to rain upon one city, and cause it not to rain upon another city.' In the second year the arrows of hunger will be sent forth. In the third a great famine; men, women, and children will die; pious men and saints (will be few), and the Law will be forgotten by its students. In the fourth, partial plenty. In the fifth, great plenty, when men will eat, drink and be merry, and the Law will return to its

---

*Notice that Rabbi Simeon uses the term *week* in this passage taken from the Talmud, just as it is used in Daniel 9:27, to indicate a seven-year period.

students. In the sixth, voices. In the seventh, wars; and at the end of the seventh year, the son of David will come." It is significant that Rabbi Simeon, whose prediction we find in the Talmud, is actually speaking of a seven-year tribulation period which will immediately precede the coming of the Messiah (Sanhedrin 97a)![18]

Rabbi Johanan said, "Wait for him [the Messiah] when you see the generations growing smaller, and many troubles coming upon Israel" (Sanhedrin 98a).

Though most of the tribulation, which Israel is to experience as a part of the birth pangs of the Messiah, is in terms of such holocaust figures as wars, disease, natural disaster, torture, and other forms of physical carnage, some rabbis had other interpretations. Rabbi Israel Ben Eliezer, for example, explained that the adversities which would befall Israel, according to the Talmud, meant that "before the coming of the Messiah, there will be a period of great prosperity and Jews will become wealthy. They will grow accustomed to extravagant living and forget all their habits of frugality. Later, a terrible depression will arise, and the means of livelihood will be scarce. Poverty will descend upon those who no longer know how to live sparingly. These will be the Messianic tribulations."

Some pious rabbis prayed that the Messiah might not come in their day in order that they might be relieved of the preadvent tribulation. Rabbi Abraham Jacob of Sadigura, during the merciless persecution of the Jews in Russia, faced this dilemma of the birth pangs of the Messiah, and prayed, "This, I am told and am inclined to believe, indicates that the labors giving birth to Redemption are upon us. But the travails are so terrible that the Jews cry unto heaven protesting their inability to sustain them. Then God in His mercy abates the pains and Redemption is delayed. Whether I pray, thus, or stay my prayer, I have reason either way to be heavy of heart." Other rabbis developed formulas for escaping this time of tribulation which would immediately precede the coming of the Messiah. When the disciples of Rabbi Eliezer asked him about this, saying, "What must a man do to be spared the pangs of the Messiah?" Rabbi Eliezer replied, "Let him busy himself with the Law and with the practice of good works." An ancient Jewish legend says that when Moses was admonishing Israel to observe the Sabbath, he promised them six gifts from God if they would be obedient, one of which is escape from the birth pangs. This is why Rabbi Simeon said that he who observes the Sabbath will be saved from three evils, one of which is the travails of the Messiah. Greenstone summarizes the characteristics of this pre-Messianic time of trouble:

> Like the early prophets and the latter apocalyptic writers, the Rabbis also taught that the Messianic period would be preceded by many tribulations, called "Messianic woes," not only for Israel, but for all the earth as well. These trials preliminary to the advent of the Messianic era will be of all kinds, social and political both. According to these teachings, there will be an increase in drunkenness and immorality. Youths will no longer respect their parents, the pious, and the aged. All family ties will be loosed, and poverty will be the portion of many. . . .Judges and officers of the law will have no authority, denunciators will multiply, anarchy will reign supreme. Even among the sages themselves there will be constant strife. The law will no longer be studied. Those that fear sin will be despised, and the house of public convention will become a house of harlots.[9]

After the period of the Talmud, the idea persisted into the Middle Ages that the coming of the Messiah would be preceded by a time of trouble for Israel. Soon after the severe persecutions of the Jews in Spain, in the year 1393, a Spanish scholar named Moses Botharel announced himself as Messiah. Reflecting upon the announcement of Botarel, and its relation to the Spanish persecution of the Jews which occured in 1391, Abraham of Granada wrote:

> And this is an indication of the approach of Redemption. When it is near, the sufferings of the exile will increase, and many of the faithful ones will stumble when they see the terrible confusion of the exile and the great sufferings, and many will leave the faith in order to escape the sword of the destroyer. . . .But blessed is the man who will cling to his faith and walk in the right path. Perhaps he will be saved from the tribulation which are called the pangs of the Messiah.[10]

The Zohar—a thirteenth-century mystical commentary on the Torah—taught that in the days of the Messiah's birth pangs there will fall upon Israel terrible calamity. All the nations of the earth will vie with each other in oppressing Israel, and "the last misfortunes shall make them forget the earlier."

The fifteenth century was a desperate century for the Jews. Expelled from Spain in 1492, their migration turned backward toward their origins. However, a hundred years before the final Spanish expulsion of the Jews, things were so desperate for these Sephardic Jews that the following picture of the horrors was recorded about the Jewish community of Castile. In it the writer likens the sorrows that he and his compatriots were enduring to the birth pangs of the Messiah. "In truth, plunders followed upon plunders, money vanished from the purse, souls from the bodies; all the sufferings that were believed to precede the Messianic period are here—but the redeemer has not come. I will not attempt to recount all the miseries; they are more numerous than sand."[11] Jewish persecutions which continued into the sixteenth and seventeenth centuries were universally interpreted as the time of trouble which would immediately precede the coming of the Messiah. The rabbis of Palestine, near the year 1648, sent an encyclical prayer out to all exilic Jewry. This prayer was to be recited at dawn and in the evening in each of the diaspora countries, and was to be accompanied by lamentations and penance. In this prayer Jews pled for the restoration of the kingdom of David and for the remission of the birth pangs of the Messianic times.

Therefore, the birth pangs of the Messiah is one of the basic elements in Jewish Messianism. In the belief that a time of hardship and testing would precede the advent of the Messiah, the Jews were enabled to accept each new crisis—as having Messianic overtones. Every succeeding generation of suffering Jews would affirm that their particular crisis could be the end time of trouble and that the Messiah's coming lay just beyond. "This conception enabled Jews to view great historical and political transformation—the fall and rise of empires and kingdoms, or revolutions and counter revolutions—as the death throes

of the fourth and last beast kingdom and the harbinger of the
Messianic eternal kingdom," says Dr. Haim Hillel Ben-
Sasson, professor of Jewish history in the Hebrew Univer-
sity in Jerusalem.[12] It was this saving formula, *chevlo shel
mashiach,* "the travail of Messiah," which enabled the
Jewish hope to prevail even in the midst of despair. Mother
Zion was a woman in travail about to give birth to a new era.

All references to the birth pangs of the Messiah which
are found in the Midrash and in the Talmud "indicate how
deeply rooted was the faith of the Jews in the ultimate
redemption and how ineradicable it has remained despite
insufferable persecutions," wrote Mordecai Kaplan. "Some
Jewish martyrs of World War II, as they were being led to
Hitler's gas chambers chanted the part of the *Ani Maamin*
credo which proclaims faith in the ultimate advent of the
Messiah."[13]

So Jewish writers in the Talmud, Midrash, and Zohar, and
even from as far back as the time of the Seleucid persecutions of Judah under Antiochus IV Epiphanes, have predicted that before the Messiah comes Israel will suffer a time
of great tribulation. Modern history has substantiated this by
demonstrating that even in the twentieth century the Jewish
people are not immune to such persecution designed to
effect their total destruction.

Does this Orthodox doctrine of the birth pangs of the
Messiah, which appears so frequently in the Midrash, the
Talmud, and other sacred Jewish literature, appear also in
Scripture? If so, can it be found in the New Testament as
well as in the Torah and the Prophets? The answer is yes, for
the Bible uniformly predicts that a time of great suffering will
be laid upon Israel just prior to the second coming of Christ.
In fact, there is no doctrine held by both Orthodox Jews and
conservative Christians which is more closely related than is
this one. The main difference is one of terminology and, of
course, the Messianic frame of reference. Orthodox Jews
use "birth pangs of the Messiah" to indicate the suffering
which will precede the (one) advent of the Messiah. Christians, who believe in the literal interpretation of Bible
prophecy, use the terminology of Jesus, who called it the
"great tribulation," and who indicated that it would occur

just prior to His own second coming (Mt 24:21, 29-30).
A divine forecast of Jewish history which includes this
idea of suffering as a prelude to Messianic restoration is
found in Deuteronomy 4:25-31:

> When thou shalt beget children, and children's children, and
> ye shall have been long in the land, and shall corrupt your-
> selves, and make a graven image in the form of anything, and
> shall do that which is evil in the sight of the LORD thy God, to
> provoke him to anger; I call heaven and earth to witness
> against you this day, that ye shall soon utterly perish from off
> the land whereunto ye go over the Jordan to possess it; ye
> shall not prolong your days upon it, but shall utterly be
> destroyed. And the LORD will scatter you among the peo-
> ples, and ye shall be left few in number among the nations,
> whither the LORD shall lead you away. And there ye shall
> serve gods, the work of men's hands, wood and stone, which
> neither see, nor hear, nor eat, nor smell. But from thence ye
> shall seek the LORD thy God, and thou shalt find him, when
> thou searchest after him with all thy heart and with all thy
> soul. *When thou art in tribulation, and all these things are
> come upon thee, in the latter days thou shalt return to the
> LORD thy God,* and hearken unto his voice: for the LORD thy
> God is a merciful God; he will not fail thee, neither destroy
> thee, nor forget the covenant of thy fathers which he sware
> unto them [italics added].

There are four elements in this divine forecast of Israel's
history. First, sin brings forfeiture of the land. This was
Israel's unique punishment.

> Because they forsook the covenant of the LORD, the God of
> their fathers, which he made with them when he brought
> them forth out of the land of Egypt, and went and served
> other gods, and worshipped them, gods that they knew not,
> and that he had not given unto them: therefore the anger of
> the LORD was kindled against this land, to bring upon it all the
> curse that is written in this book; and the LORD rooted them
> out of their land in anger, and in wrath, and in great indigna-
> tion, and cast them into another land, as at this day" (Deu
> 29:25-29).

Eretz Israel—the land of Israel—is the people's incomparable possession. To lose it is the greatest of tragedies and the most dramatic of punishment. It is said that a rabbinic friend came one day to visit Rabbi Wolf Zbaraz in Tiberias. When he came into the courtyard, he found Rabbi Zbaraz's wife hanging clothes out on a line to dry. The visiting rabbi expressed his regret that such a woman as she should have to do her own laundry. "Rabbi, the laundry is not mine," she replied. "I am washing clothes for others and they pay me to do it. But I feel no shame or regret, for no sacrifice is too great for the privilege of living in Eretz Israel!" But this privilege has been denied to the Jews for more years than it was granted. Most of the history of Israel has been a history of exile and forfeiture of the privilege of living in Eretz Israel. The sacrifice of the land was Israel's unique sorrow as a result of her sin.

Second, Moses said that scattering rather than annihilation would be a part of Israel's destiny. No other people in history have been scattered among other nations as were the Jews and yet retained their identity. They have been neither obliterated nor assimilated. They may be reduced: "ye shall be left few in number among the nations" (v. 27); but "left" they were. If the hostility of the nations threatens complete liquidation of the Jews, God has promised to stay this conspiracy by retaining a remnant among the exiles. This is why Hitler's "final solution" did not work. He could reduce the Jewish population by six million, but he could not eradicate it. Many times the prophets of Israel have noted this fact. Isaiah, for example, said,

> And it shall come to pass in that day, that the remnant of Israel and they that are escaped of the house of Jacob, shall no more again lean upon him that smote them, but shall lean upon the LORD, the Holy One of Israel, in truth. A remnant shall return, even the remnant of Jacob, unto the mighty God. For though thy people, Israel, be as the sand of the sea, only a remnant of them shall return (10:20-21).

Third, there is the promise of final regathering, based upon the covenant made with their fathers. Then fourth, there is the warning that tribulation will immediately precede this regathering. Here is one of the first places where Scripture makes mention of the suffering which will precede the Messianic age. On this foundation, the Orthodox idea of the "birth pangs of the Messiah" was built. It is on the basis of this passage in Deuteronomy, as well as others found in the Old Testament prophets and in the New Testament, that the eschatological theme of the great tribulation period, which immediately precedes the second coming of Christ, is also built (see Jer 30:4-11; Dan 12:1-2; Mt 24:21-22).

What is the purpose of the birth pangs of the Messiah, or the great tribulation as Jesus calls this time of Jewish suffering? Both Christian and Orthodox expositors agree that it is to prepare the nation Israel for the coming of the Messiah. The Jewish interpretation is that it will ready Israel for the one and only advent of the Messiah, while the New Testament indicates that it will ready Israel to accept the Lord Jesus Christ as Messiah when He comes a second time (Mt 23:37-39).

This truth is presented in one of Ezekiel's oracles, recorded in chapter 20. In this chapter the prophet deals with Israel's sin and idolatry in the past (v. 5-29) and continuing into the present (vv. 30-32). Then he looks to the future and sees that, in spite of Israel's sin, the Lord still has a purpose for His people which He will bring to fulfillment. But this ultimate fulfillment is by way of judgment and suffering on the part of the people.

> As I live, saith the Lord GOD, surely with a mighty hand, and with an outstretched arm, and with wrath poured out, will I be king over you. And I will bring you out from the peoples, and will gather you out of the countries wherein ye are scattered, with a mighty hand, and with an outstretched arm, and with wrath poured out; and I will bring you into the wilderness of the peoples, and there will I enter into judgment with you face to face. Like as I entered into judgment with your fathers in the wilderness of the land of Egypt, so will I enter into judgment with you, saith the Lord GOD. And I will cause you to pass under the rod, and I will bring you into the bond of the covenant (Eze 20:33-37).

The intent of the great tribulation period is to bring Israel to recognize the Lord Jesus Christ as her Messiah. Therefore the tribulation period has the nation Israel as its subject. It is for this reason that the church has no part in the great tribulation. The church is caught out of the world before the tribulation begins, because the church has no need of the tribulation. The church has already done voluntarily what the tribulation is designed to produce in Israel—repentance! It is for this reason that John wrote to the church in Philadelphia, "*Because* thou didst keep the word of my patience, I also will keep thee from the hour of trial, that hour which is to come upon the whole world, to try them that dwell upon the earth" (Rev 3:10, italics added). It is for the same reason that the church is not found on earth during the time of the tribulation period which is presented in Revelation 6 through 18. These chapters picture the tribulation but make absolutely no mention of the church, for the tribulation period is not designed for the church; rather it is designed for Israel and the nations. The church is removed from the earth before the tribulation begins (cf. Rev 4:1). We are now in "the year of the LORD's favor," which is the age of the church. But when the church is caught out of the world at the rapture, "the day of vengeance of our God" (Is 61:2; cf. Lk 4:19-20) will break upon the earth, and the nation Israel will be cast into great tribulation, there to experience what her sages have predicted: the birth pangs of the Messiah. As a result of this time of suffering, Israel will be brought to a knowledge of the Lord Jesus Christ as her Messiah and will accept Him as such (Zec 12:10-14; cf. Jn 19:37).

How do the birth pangs of the Messiah fit into the framework of biblical eschatology? When does this time of tribulation come upon Israel? Both Orthodox Jews and premillennial Christian expositors agree that it will occur just prior to the advent of the Messiah. The Orthodox position is no more precise than that. However, the New Testament indicates that this time of tribulation, which is designed to bring Israel to accept the Lord Jesus Christ as Messiah, begins immediately after the church is taken out of the world at the rapture, and extends to the second coming of Christ. It is also generally agreed that this period of tribulation is of seven years' duration, with the last half of this period designated the great tribulation. It is during these last three and one-half years that Israel will suffer these incomparable woes.

In fact, the Old Testament sees no break in God's dealing with the nation Israel, for the Old Testament does not view the age of the church. As for Israel during this church age, which runs its course between the cross and the rapture, Paul says that God has set Israel aside in unbelief until the church, the body of Christ, is completed (Ro 11:25). This mystery age of the church was first revealed to the apostle Paul (Eph 3:1-31; Col 1:24-29). This is why the prophet Daniel declared that seventy weeks (490 years) were determined upon Israel as the period of time in which God would fulfill his destiny for the nation Israel (Dan 9:24). Sixty-nine of these weeks (483 years) have already run their course between the time that Artaxerxes ordered the rebuilding of the walls of Jerusalem (Neh 2:1-20) in 445 B.C. and the cutting off of the Messiah—the death of the Lord Jesus Christ upon the cross (Dan 9:25-26). With sixty-nine of the weeks fulfilled, only one more is left to complete the seventy-week period. During the final week of seven years, the Lord will conclude His dealing with His covenant people, and Israel will then enter the golden age.

But was this week of God's climactic dealing with Israel fulfilled immediately after the Messiah was cut off on the cross? Did the seventieth week *immediately* follow the sixty-ninth? Obviously not. What happened? The age of the church—a great parenthesis—separates the sixty-ninth from the seventieth week. God's program for Israel as a nation was stopped at the end of the sixty-ninth week when the covenant people rejected the Lord Jesus. The nation Israel was set aside in unbelief. Then, for the last two thousand years, the age of the church—unseen in the Old Testament—has been running its course. During this time, God has been saving *individual* Gentiles and Jews who repent and believe the gospel. These individuals are added to the church, the body of Christ. The nation Israel has been dormant, as in Paul's allegory of the olive branches in Romans 11:11-24. However, when the body of Christ is complete, the Lord Jesus will return for the church, which will be

taken out of the world to meet Him in the air (1 Th 4:13-17).
It is then that the timeclock of Israel's destiny, stopped at
the cross, dormant during the entire age of the church, will
begin to tick again, and the final week of Daniel's predicted
seventy-week series will resume.

It is significant that when the timeclock ceased its movement and God's purposes for the nation Israel was frozen in
the first century at the end of the sixty-ninth week; Israel,
along with the rest of the Western world, was then under the
dominion of the Roman Empire. Two thousand years have
now passed, and the Roman Empire has disappeared from
this earthly scene. However, the prophetic Word indicates
that when the great parenthesis, the age of the church, is
fulfilled, and the seventieth week resumes its course, many
of the same political conditions will reappear. In fact, the
sure word of prophecy indicates that a revived form of the
ancient Roman Empire will again emerge in the last days.

In a series of visions recorded in Daniel 2 and 7, the
prophet sees the whole course of world events extending
from his day, during the Babylonian exile, until the second
coming of Christ, and the ushering in of the Messianic age.
Four world empires will dominate the world scene between
the sixth century B.C. when Daniel saw these visions, and
the second coming of Christ. They are Babylon, Persia,
Greece, and Rome. Because Daniel, along with all other of
the Old Testament prophets, did not see the age of the
church, he therefore views the fourth empire—Rome—in
existence at the end of the sixty-ninth week in the first
century, but also in existence when the second coming of
Christ occurs.

How is this extension possible, since the western division of the Roman Empire collapsed in the fifth century A.D.
and the eastern division passed from the scene of world
history several centuries later? Furthermore, how is this
possible, seeing that the age of the church is still running its
course today, long after the ancient Roman Empire disappeared? The answer is that the mystery age of the church is a
vast parenthesis in history, injected between the ancient
Roman Empire of the first century, and the revived Roman
Empire of the last days. Therefore the prophetic Scriptures

indicate that there will be some form of the revived Roman Empire on the world scene when the second coming of Christ occurs. Furthermore, it is this resurgent Roman Empire which will be the dominant political force during the tribulation period. In addition, at its head will be a new Caesar, a world dictator whom the Bible identifies as the Antichrist.

Therefore when the prophetic timeclock stopped in God's dealing with the nation Israel after the sixty-ninth week, at that point in the first century when the Messiah was cut off on the cross, the nation Israel was under the control of the Roman Empire. The people of Israel, after the Great Revolt, were scattered to the ends of the earth. Rome finally disappeared from history. However, during the last days, just prior to the tribulation period, God's covenant people will be regathered back to the land. Even today we have seen the State of Israel reconstituted. After the church is caught out at the rapture, ending the great parenthesis, the revived Roman Empire will emerge. The prophetic timeclock will begin again to tick off the final seventieth week in God's dealing with His covenant people Israel. However, Israel will not only be back in the land when this occurs, but the Roman Empire will be revived, and therefore political conditions will be just as they were two thousand years ago when the sixty-ninth week was concluded and God terminated His dealing with Israel nationally during the first century!

It is extremely significant that many of the most responsible observers today see world conditions adjusting themselves in a way that is highly reminiscent of the first century. Professors Herman Kahn and Anthony Wiener of the Hudson Institute have written, "Nevertheless we would suggest that some of the prospects for the year 2000 are, in effect, a return to a sort of new Augustinian age. . . .While the issues of cause and effect are complicated and inherently inconclusive, there are some parallels between Roman times and ours. Various analogies, however trite or inaccurate in their usual formulations, ought not be dismissed without some thought, at least as sources for conjectures."[14] They first note the parallel between the increase of leisure which occurred in the first century and that of our own day. When

Augustus came to power, the free citizens of Rome had seventy-six holidays a year. By the time of Nero a hundred more had been added. In our world, productivity rises by three or four percent per hour, so that the more that is produced, the more that can be produced. When more and more is produced, with less and less time and energy required, the result is that more leisure becomes available. A leisure which characterized the Roman world is emerging to characterize our world also. But further, in discussing current culture, Kahn and Weiner say, "something very much like our multifold trend occurred in Hellenistic Greece, the late Roman Republic, and the early Roman Empire."[15] As evidence of this, they note the parallels between the contemporary increase of secular culture, the advance of technology, the rise of education and affluence, along with an expanding urbanization. Both the Roman world and our world are marked by an aura of rapid change.

Professor Howard Snyder also notes a number of other things in our world which he believes parallels the first-century Roman Empire. First, the Roman world and our world is essentially an urban world, with cities playing the major cultural role. Of the sixty million who populated the Roman Empire, he calculates that fifteen percent lived in the major cities of one hundred thousand or more. Rome was the largest first-century city, with a population of around a million. In the remaining smaller cities, about one-half of the population lived. This situation was to change radically during the ensuing Middle Ages. These cities determined the cultural life of the ancient Roman Empire, as the urban areas do today in our society. Second, the Pax Romana provided for political unity and stability. In spite of some local conflicts, Snyder contends that our world is generally one which gives promise of decreasing, rather than increasing hostility. Such things as the fear of a nuclear holocaust, the presence of American military might all over the world, plus the influence of the United Nations, are cited as possible factors in maintaining this world stability. Snyder calls these the functional equivalent of the Pax Romana. Admittedly, this is not as convincing as some of the other parallels he draws.

Third, he notes the worldwide spread of one dominant

culture and language. Just as Kóine Greek was the lingua franca of the Roman world, so English is the one most significant vehicle of cultural dissemination in our world today. That culture is Western—even American—just as Hellenistic culture was predominant in the ancient world. Hellenism had been on the rise since the time of Alexander the Great in the fourth century B.C.; and though Rome conquered the world in the first century, Greek ideas conquered the Roman world. Another parallel between the two eras is that of international travel, communication and cultural interchange. The fifty-two thousand miles of Roman roads, many of which remain today, made possible the secure exchange of goods and services. The parallel between the rapid dissemination of culture in the ancient world and in our world is too obvious to need elaboration. Again, the one world outlook which locks all of mankind into a common destiny was at least latent in the first century, as it is patent in our world. In the first century there was also widespread religious and philosophical ferment. The old religious beliefs were being contested and were breaking down. Mystery religions arose, along with the rapid spread of the gospel of Christ. The parallel between this and the present world is most impressive. Then, finally, there is the oft-mentioned parallel between our world and the moral breakdown of the Roman Empire.[16]

All these similarities could indicate that the stage is even now being set for the revival of the Roman Empire. Though the substance—the emergence of revived Rome— will not appear until after the rapture of the church, its shadow may be falling across the world scene even today. At any rate, it is in the framework of the Roman Empire that the birth pangs of the Messiah will be executed.

The birth pangs of the Messiah will be manifest in connection with the Roman Empire which will again be upon the world scene. In fact, it is revived Rome which will inflict this time of tribulation upon Israel, just as ancient Rome inflicted untold horror upon ancient Israel. It is interesting that the rabbis of the second century believed that the fall of Rome was a necessary prerequisite to the establishment of the Messianic kingdom. The disciples of Rabbi Jose Ben Kisma asked him, "When will the Son of David come?" He answered, "I fear lest you demand a sign of me." They said to him, "We will demand no sign of you." So he answered them, "When the gate [of Caesarea Philippi] falls down, is rebuilt, falls again, and is again rebuilt, and again falls—they will not have time to rebuild it [a third time] before the Son of David comes." They said to him, "Master, give us a sign." He protested, "Did you not assure me that you would not demand a sign?" They replied, "Nevertheless, we desire one." He said to them, "Very well, let the waters of the cave of Pamias be turned into blood." And they were turned into blood (Sanhedrin 98*ab*).

The cave of Pamias is near Caesarea Philippi. In ancient times it was near the northernmost point in Palestine. Thus the gate of Caesarea Philippi was the gate through which invaders came to the land. The fall of the gates several times indicates that the Romans, then in power, would be defeated by invading armies but would recover each time. Finally the Romans would be overcome, and the way would be prepared for the coming of the Messiah. So the rabbis speculated. This Talmudic theory has an interesting parallel in Bible prophecy. The Messiah could not come, in ancient rabbinic belief, until Rome be fallen. However, this is exactly what the prophetic Word indicates will happen during the tribulation period. It will be the revived Roman Empire which will inflict the birth pangs of the Messiah upon Israel, and it will be the fall of the revived Roman Empire which will occur at the second coming of Christ and the ushering in of the Messianic kingdom (cf. Dan 2:44-45). "Several things are hidden from men," says the Talmud. "These are the day of death, the day of consolation [resurrection], the depth of judgment; no man knows what is in the mind of his friend, no man knows which of his business ventures will be profitable, or when the kingdom of the house of David will be restored, or when the sinful kingdom will fall" (Pesachim 54*b*). The rabbis speculated that the restoration of the house of David would be connected with the fall of the "sinful kingdom," the Roman Empire. And so it will be. Though this *Baraita* had ancient Rome in view, in actual prophetic fact, Israel will not be established again under David's greater Son, the Lord

Jesus Christ, until the revived Roman Empire has arisen and then fallen.

It is the suffering of the Jew during the tribulation period, known to the sages as the birth pangs of the Messiah, which will bring the nation Israel to accept the Lord Jesus as the true Messiah. Even Herzl saw the inseparable relationship between suffering and the Messianic ideal—though he would hardly have used that terminology. Herzl's fundamental conception of the Jewish state as outlined in his *Judenstaat*, is based upon the wretched plight of the Jew in eastern Europe during the late nineteenth century. Herzl's Zionist ideology was related to anti-Semitism, for he believed that this would be the thing that would finally drive the Jews back to the land. He quite frankly confessed that this was the only motive sufficient to impel the Jewish masses to attempt a return. It is not only their suffering that drives them back to the land, but it will be their suffering in the tribulation that will drive Israel to her final spiritual solution—Jesus the Messiah.

How does this come about? The Jews, whom Adolph Hitler called "the world-poisoners," survived him. His racial laws did not achieve their ends. The war had not meant, as Hitler prophesied on January 30, 1939, "the annihilation of the Jewish race throughout Europe." The death of the six million had not hidden his failure at genocide, even from Hitler himself. In fact, if Hitler had lived only three years longer, he would have learned the most astounding truth: His holocaust had made possible the thing that he hated and feared the most—a sovereign Jewish state! By 1947 the Jews were in the Holy Land in such quantities and with such political strength as to threaten the British Mandate. This, in turn, necessitated the decision of the United Nations which brought about the partition of Palestine and created the new State of Israel.

Though the return of the Jews to the land has providential overtones, this current return is not to be confused with the great Messianic regathering which will issue in the spiritual regeneration of Israel. The new State of Israel is the most important prophetic event to occur since the Great Revolt.

However, it only sets the stage for the Messianic events of the last days. The real significance of the new State of Israel is that it will greatly facilitate the rapid fulfillment of prophecy during the tribulation period. Therefore, the new State of Israel is a basic premise to the prophetic events which are to follow.

One more predicted event must transpire before the resurgence of the Roman Empire in the last days. This is the removal of the true church, the body of Christ, from this world scene. Only then can the sinister figure appear who will head up the revived Roman Empire (2 Th 2:1-3). When the church is caught out of the world to meet the Lord in the air, then the rise of the Antichrist will occur.

It is predictable that world chaos will result at the rapture of the church due to the sudden disappearance of every born-again Christian from the earth. Nearly every country will lose some leaders who are Christians when Jesus returns for the church. However, in those countries of the Western world where there are many Christian leaders in industry, the military, the professions, education, business, science, as well as among the masses of common workers, many people will suddenly disappear. Since there are more Christians in the occidental world than there are in any other society, western Europe and the United States will be the most weakened by this sudden event. It is this chaos in Western society which becomes the melee out of which the Antichrist arises. Apparently, just after the rapture there will be ten national leaders, located within the boundary of the ancient Roman Empire, who will form a coalition. There is a power struggle within this coalition in which three of these kings are subdued (Dan 7:20, 24). At this point, early in the tribulation period, a strong figure will emerge. The name which John uses in his epistles, "antichrist," has been generally accepted as the one name which best identifies him. Therefore, the Antichrist will emerge out of this ten-nation confederation as a new Caesar, the absolute ruler of the revived Roman Empire.

During the first half of the tribulation period the Antichrist will deal equitably with Israel. Under the terms of a covenant made with the Jews, the Antichrist will allow the temple to be rebuilt and the Levitical sacrificial system to begin again (Dan 9:27; 12:11). Just as in the first century, Israel will again become an affiliate of the Roman Empire. During this time Israel will prosper under the covenant protection of the Antichrist. They will dwell securely in unwalled cities, says the prophet Ezekiel (38:8, 10, 14).

But suddenly, at midtribulation, the Antichrist will turn upon Israel, break the covenant (Dan 9:27) and plunge Israel into her final holocaust—the birth pangs of the Messiah. Jesus said of this time, "for then shall be great tribulation, such as hath not been from the beginning of the world until now, no, nor ever shall be. And except those days had been shortened, no flesh would have been saved: but for the elect's sake those days shall be shortened" (Mt 24:21-22). The elect is the nation Israel. God will temper this time of tribulation to endure just long enough to accomplish its aim—to ready Israel to accept Jesus as Messiah. The prophet Isaiah used a parable in one of his oracles uttered against Judah during the Assyrian crisis. Even while predicting the judgment of God upon Judah, Isaiah, in his parable of the farmer, indicated that God would allow only enough suffering to accomplish remedial ends. "For he will not be always threshing it: and though the wheel of his cart and his horses scatter it, he doth not grind it. This also cometh forth from the LORD of hosts, who is wonderful in counsel, and excellent in wisdom" (Is 28:28-29). So the wisdom of God will determine the extent of the suffering which His covenant people will endure during the great tribulation.

Just as the Jews fled from persecution during the Great Revolt and from the Russian pogroms and the Nazi Holocaust, the great tribulation will again be a time of fleeing for Israel. Jesus said, "When therefore ye see the abomination of desolation, which was spoken of through Daniel the prophet, standing in the holy place (let him that readeth understand), then let them that are in Judea flee unto the mountains: let him that is on the housetop not go down to take out the things that are in his house: and let him that is in the field not return back to take his cloak. But woe unto them that are with child and to them that give suck in those days! And pray ye that your flight be not in the winter, neither on a sabbath" (Mt 24:15-20).

It is worth noting that the Jews were the first people in history to be persecuted for purely religious reasons. This occurred in the second century B.C. when Antiochus IV Epiphanes, the ruler of the Syrian Seleucid dynasty which dominated Judah, attempted to force Hellenism upon the Jews. Professor Zeitlin says, "These Judaeans who willingly faced torture and death for their belief in God were the first martyrs in history."[17] The Jews will also be the last people in history to be persecuted for religious reasons. The Antichrist will attempt to force the cult of the Beast upon them and to coerce them to abandon their ancient faith and worship him as god. During the persecutions of Antiochus IV, many Jews fled Judea. Some fled to Egypt where the son of Onias III had founded a sanctuary near present-day Cairo. Others fled to the wilderness of Judea where they found refuge in caves. Perhaps Hebrews 11:37-38 refers to them.

But the prophetic word indicates the Jews will flee to the east during the persecutions of the Antichrist. At first this is puzzling, for nothing lies east of Jerusalem but the arid wastes of the wilderness of Judea. From the Mount of Olives, looking eastward, all one can see is the great void that stretches between the city and the Dead Sea. However, this rugged wilderness at the back door of Jerusalem has been for centuries an area of refuge for the Jews during times of persecution. This is particularly so during the days of the Great Revolt and again after the fall of Bethar in A.D. 135. Down the Jericho road, toward the Dead Sea, the survivors of Titus' siege of Jerusalem fled to take refuge at Masada. A generation later, the followers of Simon Bar Kokhba fled down the Valley of Fire to seek refuge in the caves, which only recently have begun to yield their archaeological treasures—the remains of these refugees.

In Revelation, John says, "the woman[Israel] fled into the wilderness, where she hath a place prepared of God, that there they may nourish her a thousand two hundred and threescore days [three and one-half years]" (12:6, cf. v. 14). Many identify this place as the ancient city of Petra south of the Dead Sea. It may refer to the whole territory which makes up Transjordan, or even to other locations for that matter, because Matthew 25:31-46 indicates that the nations will be judged at the second coming of Christ according to the way that they deal with Israel during this time when she is fleeing from the wrath of the Antichrist. During the Nazi Holocaust, the world conveniently ignored the plight of the Jew. Much of the world may do so again during the great tribulation. However, for those nations who do provide protection and sustenance for fleeing Israel, there is promised a special blessing.

During this time, Israel will not only suffer intense physical deprivation and persecution, but the Jews will endure the agony of spiritual assault. The spiritual agony will come from three sources. First, the ancient Levitical system, centered in the sanctuary, the priesthood, and the offerings, so dear to Orthodox Jews, will again be denied them. Having begun only recently in the rebuilt temple, the sacrifices will cease when the Antichrist breaks his covenant with Israel (Dan 9:27; 12:11). Second, the Antichrist will force all people to worship him as god. Those who refuse will be killed (Rev 13:7-8, 12, 15). Third, during this time there will appear false messiahs who will attempt to delude Israel. Jesus gave clear warning of this:

> Then if any man shall say unto you, Lo, here is the Christ, or, Here; believe it not. For there shall arise false Christs, and false prophets, and shall show great signs and wonders; so as to lead astray, if possible, even the elect. Behold, I have told you beforehand. If therefore they shall say unto you, Behold, he is in the wilderness; go not forth: Behold, he is in the inner chambers; believe it not. For as the lightning cometh forth from the east, and is seen even unto the west; so shall be the coming of the Son of man (Mt 24:23-27).

The Antichrist will not be a false Messiah. Rather, his purpose is to force all mankind to worship him as god. However, there will be numerous false messiahs who will appear during the great tribulation period, just as false messiahs emerged during Israel's travail at the time of the Great Revolt in the first century.

The Hasidic rabbis tell that on one occasion, an unbeliever accused Rabbi Akiba of being steeped in error because he believed that Bar Kokhba was the Messiah. In defense of Rabbi Akiba, the Hasidic Rabbi of Berditschev told the following parable. Once upon a time, when the son of a mighty emperor became ill, various physicians were consulted. One advised that the bare body of the boy be covered with a burning salve and then wrapped in linen cloth. However, another physician rejected this idea because the son of the emperor was too ill to endure the pain. Another physician suggested a sleeping potion be given the boy, while still another noted doctor objected that this might endanger the weakened heart of the patient. At this point, a fifth physician suggested that the boy be sedated, wrapped in the burning salve, and as often as he awakened thereafter, be given additional spoonfuls of sleeping-drought. And so it was done. Then the rabbi said, "When God saw that Israel was sick he wrapped it in the biting linen of poverty and misery, but he also laid upon Israel the sleep of forgetfulness in order that it might endure the pain. But, lest Israel expire completely, God awakens it from hour to hour with the false hope of a Messiah and again lets Israel return to sleep until the night of suffering be over and the true Messiah be come!"[18] Perhaps it really is the appearance of false messiahs which has kept alive the Messianic hope in Israel and will do so again during the tribulation period (cf. Mt 24:5, 11, 23-26).

The resilient Judaism which survives the tribulation will form the matrix out of which Jews will finally come to a knowledge of their true Messiah.

A few days after the Americans captured Buchenwald, the loud speaker announced that the Jewish chaplain in the United States forces would conduct services for the festival of *Shabuoth* (Pentecost), which marks the anniversary of the giving of the law on Mount Sinai. What would be the attitude of the Jews—those physical and mental cripples who had survived the unprecedented horror of the death camps? Had these survivors of the Nazi hell been completely relieved of any faith in the covenant God of their fathers? Would the thousands of haunted souls for whom religion had done so little to prevent the horror, respond to this challenge to attend religious services in order to commemorate the receiving of the Torah by the nation long ago?

That night thousands of Jews, in a vast demonstration of faith and loyalty to God, gathered to attend the first Jewish religious services to be held upon the soil of defeated Germany. One who was there writes:

> The cripples, the injured, and the weak came to demonstrate to the world that the last ounce of their strength, the last drop of their blood, and the last breath of their lives belonged to God, to Torah, and to the Jewish religion. As Chaplain Schechter intoned the Evening Prayers, all the inmates in and outside the block stood in silence, re-accepting the Torah whose people, message, and purpose Hitler's Germany had attempted to destroy. Jewish history repeated itself. Just as our forefathers who were liberated from Egypt accepted the Law in the desert, so did we, the liberated Jews of Buchenwald, re-accept the same Law in the concentration camps of Germany.[19]

But this is only a preview of how the orthodox Jewish spirit will respond to the horrors of the great tribulation period, which will neither completely destroy the Jew nor utterly demoralize him. He will survive the tribulation holocaust, his orthodox frame of reference intact. But then a great difference will occur. Where the European Jews survived the Nazi Holocaust to reaffirm their ancient faith, the remnant of Jewish survivors of the great tribulation period will come to a new and glorious experience. The prophet Zechariah predicted the outcome of the great tribulation period for the Jew:

> And I will pour upon the house of David, and upon the inhabitants of Jerusalem, the spirit of grace and of supplication; and they shall look unto me whom they have pierced; and they shall mourn for him, as one mourneth for his only son (Zec 12:10).

As a result of the suffering of the great tribulation, the surviving Jews will accept the One whom their fathers pierced upon the cross centuries ago.

> And so all Israel shall be saved: even as it is written, There shall come out of Zion the Deliverer; He shall turn away

ungodliness from Jacob: And this is my covenant unto them, When I shall take away their sins. As touching the gospel, they are enemies for your sake: but as touching the election, they are beloved for the fathers' sake. For the gifts and the calling of God are not repented of. For as ye in time past were disobedient to God, but now have obtained mercy by their disobedience, even so have these also now been disobedient, that by the mercy shown to you they also may now obtain mercy. For God hath shut up all unto disobedience, that he might have mercy upon all. O the depth of the riches both of the wisdom and the knowledge of God! how unsearchable are his judgments, and his ways past tracing out! For who hath known the mind of the Lord? or who hath been his counsellor? or who hath first given to him, and it shall be recompensed unto him again? For of him, and through him, and unto him, are all things. To him be the glory for ever. Amen (Ro 11:26-36).

5

THE COMING OF ISRAEL'S MESSIAH

Oh! Weep for those that wept by Babel's stream,
Whose shrines are desolate, whose land a dream;
Weep for the harp of Judah's broken shell;
Mourn—where their God hath dwelt the godless dwell!

And where shall Israel lave her bleeding feet?
And where shall Zion's song again seem sweet?
And Judah's melody once more rejoice
The hearts that leap'd before its heavenly voice?

Tribes of the wandering foot and weary breast
How shall ye flee away and be at rest!
The wild-dove hath her nest, the fox his cave,
Mankind their country—Israel but the grave!

So wrote Lord Bryon in his "Hebrew Melodies." For centuries the path which Israel trod led only to an anonymous grave. But it will not always be so. The Hebrew prophets proclaimed that a day is coming when Israel will not only be gathered back to the land, but she will also have a King in David's line ruling upon the throne from the city of Jerusalem which is destined to become the capital of the world! For this the Jews have prayed ever since Nebuchadnezzar removed the last king in the line of David from the throne, reduced the temple to ashes, sacked the city, and transported the people around the Fertile Crescent to Babylon.

An ancient Jewish legend records that in a certain place there were several pieces of fine lumber lying in the muddy ground. No one paid any attention to them until one day a skilled cabinet maker happened to pass that way and recognized their worth. He purchased these boards from their neglectful owner and made them into beautiful pieces of furniture. When the former owner of the lumber saw these objects, he said regretfully, "I considered the wood worthless, yet behold what beautiful things have been fashioned from it." By the same token, says this legend, the Egyptians, the Assyrians, the Babylonians, as well as the Seleucids and the Romans, have forced Israel to live in degradation, and to occupy themselves with low trades. But when they see the beauty of Israel emancipated, they will regret their treatment of her and will be compelled to offer admiration.

The book of Isaiah closes with the declaration that the name of Israel and her seed will remain before the Lord forever (66:22). This reconfirms the fact that God has a purpose for the covenant people of Israel that was neither qualified by Israel's faithfulness nor revoked by her sin. To be sure, the sin of Israel delayed the fulfillment of this covenant purpose, even as her arch sin—the rejection of the Lord Jesus Christ as Messiah—necessitated the setting aside of Israel in unbelief for many centuries; yet the final purpose of God for Israel has never been aborted.

This unalterable purpose of God for Israel has been confirmed to us in two different ways: first, through the terms of the covenant made with the nation; and second, by the pragmatic facts of history.

In chapter three we dealt with the first of these unalterable confirmations when we looked at the content of the covenant made with Abraham, recorded in Genesis 12:1-3. Now one further note is necessary. We need to observe the working of this covenant in history. Why has Israel suffered exile from the land when the covenant made unconditional promises that Abraham and his seed would possess the land forever? The nature of the covenant is such that there were within its *unconditional* framework certain *conditions* which Israel must fulfill in order to perpetuate her temporal blessings in the land. At any given moment, Israel may suffer exile from the land as a punishment for disobedience. However, that exile can never be permanent, for Israel will ultimately possess the land as a result of the unconditional promises contained in the original covenant made with Abraham.

Therefore God's dealing with the nation has two main features. One is the *unconditional* affirmation of the Abrahamic covenant, in which Israel is promised the land as an eternal heritage. But within the framework of this covenant there are also to be found the *conditional* stipulations of the Sinai covenant in which God promised a sustained blessing for the people in the land only as a result of their obedience to His commands. If they disobey, they will be temporarily exiled from the land as the unique punishment for their sin. And this is just what the history of Israel has demonstrated. She suffered periodic exile from the land for violating the conditional terms of the Sinai covenant. Though the last exile has lasted for almost two thousand years, Israel will be regathered finally to possess the land under the unconditional terms of the Abrahamic covenant. This is why each of the two covenants is marked by a key formula. The Abrahamic covenant (Gen 12:1-3, 6-7; 13:14-17; 15:1-21; 17:1-18; 22:15-18) is marked by the unconditional key formula, "I will" (cf. also Deu 30:1-10; 2 Sa 7:10-16; Jer 31:31-40). The other, the Sinai covenant, is marked by the conditional key formula, "*If* you will, *then* I will." (Ex 19:5ff; Deu 28:1-68).

It was this unconditional covenant that was in view when God spoke to Abraham and said,

> And I will establish my covenant between me and thee and thy seed after thee throughout their generations for an everlasting covenant, to be a God unto thee and to thy seed after thee. And I will give unto thee, and to thy seed after thee, the land of thy sojournings, all the land of Canaan, for an everlasting possession; and I will be their God (Gen 17:7-8).

But it was the conditional covenant which was later applied to the seed of Abraham at Mount Sinai that is in view when the Lord said to Solomon on the occasion of the dedication of the first temple,

> But if ye shall turn away from following me, ye or your children, and not keep my commandments and my statutes which I have set before you, but shall go and serve other gods, and worship them; then will I cut off Israel out of the land which I have given them; and this house, which I have hallowed for my name, will I cast out of my sight; and Israel shall be a proverb and a byword among all peoples. And though this house is so high, yet shall every one that passeth by it be astonished, and shall hiss; and they shall say, Why hath the LORD done thus unto this land, and to this house? and they shall answer Because they forsook the LORD their God, who brought forth their fathers out of the land of Egypt, and laid hold on other gods, and worshipped them, and served them: therefore hath the LORD brought all this evil upon them (1 Ki 9:6-9).

There is a second confirmation of this truth concerning God's ultimate purpose for Israel. It is seen in the pragmatic strategems of history which have conspired for two thousand years toexterminate the Jew, but have failed. Neither the scimitar of Islam, the sword of the Crusaders, the rack of the inquisitors, the pogroms of the Russians, the gas chambers of the Nazis, nor the Holy War of the modern Arabs have been able to eradicate the Jew.

Only the Jew refused to fit neatly into Toynbee's theory of the rise and fall of a people. The great English historian relegates the Jews to a footnote, in which he calls them the fossils of history because Israel would not join the other nations in civilization's inevitable flow toward oblivion. In discussing the Jew, Toynbee uses the term *fossil remnant* numerous times in his monumental work, *A Study of History.* He does not define this term which he applies to the Jewish people, but he apparently means the same thing which the scientist means by *fossil.* A fossil is something hard and petrified: a shell, once animated by life but now adamant, rigid, and inflexible—a frozen form from the past. Toynbee calls the Jewish community a "fossil relic of a dead civilization" and an "archaism." As for Zionism, which created the new State of Israel, Toynbee feels that, though the idea of restoration is inherent in Jewish nationalism, it should have been left to the divine will to execute. He condemns political Zionism as having been seized by western-type initiative which infused the Jewish desire for a national homeland with aggressive action in the fulfillment of this ideal. Thus, Toynbee says, Zionism became guilty of perverting the divine plan for restoration, just as Communism is guilty of perverting the divine plan for utopianism. Zionism is a usurpation of divine providence. He concedes the success of Zionism but attributes this success to the power of American Jewry, the Nazi attempt at genocide, and the cold war. While Toynbee concedes to an idealized future for Israel, he eliminates any divine purpose from the events of 1948.[1]

There are only two sizeable groups of Jews remaining in the diaspora today. One is in the Soviet Union. The other is in the United States. As these words are being written, those Jews in the USSR want to leave but cannot. The Jews in the United States can leave but will not. The Soviet Jews will resist the attempt of the Russian government to stamp out their culture, their life style, and their religion. This is an old story with predictable results. If the Soviet policy toward the Jews becomes the extermination policy of Hitler, Russian Jewry may be reduced to a nonentity. If the policy is one of discrimination and restriction only, the Jews of Russia will survive—but with great suffering and physical loss, as their ancestors have endured and survived Russian pogroms before.

But what of the Jewish community in America? Professor Earl Raab of the University of California suggests several alternatives: (1) aliyah—Jews go to Israel; (2) extension—Jews live in America as a cultural and emotional extension of Jewish life in Israel; (3) authenticity—Jews live in America with a special identity and authenticity as American Jews; (4) disappearance—Jews gradually disappear as Jews in America.[2] Many believe that American Jewry will finally assimilate itself out of existence. This will come about through intermarriage, secularization, and social integration. As external pressures are reduced, so will the unique identity of the Jew. The only bulwark against assimilation in American Jewry is Orthodox Judaism which perpetuates the traits which have tended to keep the Jew separate and viable in the past. Since Reform Judaism has none of these peculiar restrictions, assimilation is practically guaranteed among them.

Though assimilation and pogroms may take their toll, a remnant of Jews have always survived the conspiracies of history and will continue to do so until the Messiah comes. The twentieth century has seen history's most determined attempt to eradicate the covenant people. Only the great tribulation period will rival the Nazi Holocaust in intensity. However, Israel has been exposed to many formal threats to its existence in the past. Max Dimont's brilliant and fascinating book, *Jews, God and History* is built around six challenges which history has hurled at the Jew. The first is the challenge of the pagan world. Israel occupied a narrow land bridge which ran between the Mediterranean Sea and the Arabian Desert, connecting Africa with Europe and Asia. Across this narrow corridor the armies of the nations march in order to engage one another in battle. Often these battles took place on this narrow land bridge itself, threatening the Jews who occupied it. The second threat was Greek culture and Roman imperialism. The Greeks, especially the Seleucids, determined to crush out the uniqueness of Judaism by imposing Hellenism upon the Jews, while the Romans determined to stamp out the Jew through military might. Both Antiochus IV Epiphanes and the emperor Hadrian, the arch representatives of each of these attempts at spiritual and physical genocide, failed. Third, there was Israel's unique threat—exile and its attendant danger of assimilation. Israel's refusal to be absorbed into the people among whom she was scattered is unparalleled in history.

The fourth threat was the growth of Islam. For over seven hundred years the Jews endured the threat of Islamic culture, even prospering within its domain, for in these centuries of Moorish dominion in Africa and Europe, the Jews reached new peaks of intellectual endeavor, becoming statesmen, philosophers, physicians, scientists, businessmen, and cosmopolitan capitalists. The fifth challenge was the Middle Ages and Christianity. Forced conversion was resisted, and the Inquisition was endured. Yet Israel survived. The sixth challenge is that of modern anti-Semitism which climaxed in the Nazi Holocaust. Often the rabbis likened Israel to sand, on the basis of Genesis 32:12, "I will surely do thee good, and make thy seed as the sand of the sea, which cannot be numbered for multitude." Rabbi Jacob Joseph HaKohen once said that sand is distinct, and only when it passes through fire does it become glass. Likewise the Israelites are usually divided until the fire of calamity unites them into one. Israel's troubles have only served to unite and to perpetuate her as a unique and viable entity.

But for what purpose?

The Talmud says that God wears phylacteries on His forehead and on His hand, whereupon are written the words, "Who is like unto Thy people, Israel, one nation?" God's perpetual care for Israel is based upon His electing love for her, which will not be requited until Israel is back in the land under the spiritual dominion of the Messiah. In the beginning God chose Israel. "For thou art a holy people unto the Lord thy God: The Lord they God hath chosen thee to be a people for his own possession, above all peoples that are upon the face of the earth" (Deu 7:6; cf. 1 Ki 8:53; Amos 3:2). However, this election of Israel, which first set aside the nation for the Lord's purposes, will also guarantee final fulfillment of this purpose for her. "For the Lord will have compassion on Jacob, and will yet choose Israel, and set them in their own land: and the sojourner shall join himself with them, and they shall cleave to the house of Jacob" (Is 14:1). "Thus saith the Lord of hosts: My cities shall yet overflow with prosperity: and the Lord shall yet comfort Zion, and shall yet choose Jerusalem" (Zec 1:17). This is why Paul affirms that "all Israel shall be saved. . . .For the gifts and the calling of God are not repented of" (Ro 11:26, 29).

Snaith says, "The one thing of which all Old Testament writers are certain is that God's love for Israel was not because of anything that Israel had done or was."[3] Over and over again the writer of Deuteronomy proclaims that Israel had no merit of her own. It was not Israel's righteousness that determined the choice of God (Deu 7:7-8; 9:4-5; cf. Is 48:9; Jer 14:7, 21; Eze 20:9, 22, 44).

Therefore, the electing love of God for Israel must be

understood in terms, not of what Israel was, but what Israel was to become. Though the people of Israel have steadfastly refused to conform voluntarily to what God intended for them in the course of history, ultimately His purpose will be fulfilled. Though much of God's purpose for Israel can be found revealed in her past history (cf. Ro 3:1-2; 9:1-5), God's purpose for Israel is not finally understood in the historical terms of election. God's purpose must be finally read in terms of Israel's eschatology—what she is yet to become for the glory of God. Thus the prophet Isaiah said,

> Fear not; for I am with thee: I will bring thy seed from the east, and gather thee from the west; I will say to the north, Give up; and to the south, Keep not back; bring my sons from far, and my daughters from the end of the earth; every one that is called by my name, and whom I have created for my glory, whom I have formed, yea, whom I have made (43:5-7).
>
> Sing, O ye heavens, for the LORD hath done it; shout, ye lower parts of the earth; break forth into singing, ye mountains, O forest, and every tree therein: for the LORD hath redeemed Jacob, and will glorify himself in Israel (44:23).

Israel's privileged position was a result of God's arbitrary choice. Her fulfilled destiny will also be the result of this same arbitrary working of God. This is the reason why Israel's final acceptance of Jesus as Messiah is declared in the prophetic word as a fact and not merely as a hopeful speculation.

The prophet Isaiah gave another reason for Israel's election. He declares that God's choice of Israel will also benefit the Gentiles, for in the Messianic age Israel will be a light to the nations.

> I, the LORD, have called thee in righteousness, and will hold thy hand, and will keep thee, and give thee for a covenant of the people, for a light of the Gentiles; to open the blind eyes, to bring out the prisoners from the dungeon, and them that sit in darkness out of the prison-house. I am the LORD, that is my name; and my glory will I not give to another, neither my praise unto graven images (Is 42:6-8).

Some of the rabbis were not willing to concede that there will be a place for the Gentiles in the Messiah's kingdom. The Talmud says, "No proselytes will be accepted in the Days of the Messiah, just as no proselytes were accepted in the days of David or in the days of Solomon" (Yebamoth 24b), for just as in the days of David and Solomon, Gentiles might have become converted not out of conviction, but in order to gain material and political advantage, so in the Messianic age. However, there were other rabbis who believed that the blessings of the Messianic age would be extended to all people—except the Romans! Rabbi Simon Ben-Gamaliel II said, "In Jerusalem all nations and all kingdoms are destined to be gathered together, as it is written, 'At that time they shall call Jerusalem the throne of the LORD; and all the nations shall be gathered unto it' (Jer. 3:17)." However, Rabbi Ishmael quoted his father, Rabbi Jose, as declaring that the Romans would be rejected by the Messiah-King, saying, "But the Holy One, blessed be He, will say to Gabriel: 'Rebuke the wild beast [which he interpreted to be Rome] of the reeds, the multitude of the bulls,' Psm. 68:30."

The purpose of God in electing Israel is that she might take the message of God's redeeming love to the nonelect. Paul summarizes the privileged position of Israel in the purpose of God when he said:

> I say the truth in Christ, I lie not, my conscience bearing witness with me in the Holy Spirit, that I have great sorrow and unceasing pain in my heart. For I could wish that I myself were anathema from Christ for my brethren's sake, my kinsmen according to the flesh: who are Israelites; whose is the adoption, and the glory, and the covenants, and the giving of the law, and the service of God, and the promises; whose are the fathers, and of whom is Christ as concerning the flesh, who is over all, God blessed for ever (Ro 9:1-5).

Israel failed in this mission, and God set her aside in unbelief (Ro 11:25). For the last two thousand years the church has been bearing the gospel message of God's redeeming love to the world. However, God has one final eschatological purpose for Israel. He will redeem her both physically and spiritually in order that He might demonstrate finally and conclusively what His purposes for Israel could have meant all along, if they had only obeyed. The prophet Ezekiel put it this way:

> Therefore say unto the house of Israel, Thus saith the Lord GOD: I do not this for your sake, O house of Israel, but for my holy name, which ye have profaned among the nations, whither ye went. And I will sanctify my great name, which hath been profaned among the nations, which ye have profaned in the midst of them; and the nations shall know that I am the LORD, saith the Lord GOD, when I shall be sanctified in you before their eyes. For I will take you from among the nations, and gather you out of all the countries, and will bring you into your own land. And I will sprinkle clean water upon you, and ye shall be clean: from all your filthiness, and from all your idols, will I cleanse you. A new heart also will I give you, and a new spirit will I put within you; and I will take away the stony heart out of your flesh, and I will give you a heart of flesh. And I will put my Spirit within you, and cause you to walk in my statutes, and ye shall keep mine ordinances, and do them. And ye shall dwell in the land that I gave to your fathers; and ye shall be my people, and I will be your God. And I will save you from all your uncleannesses: and I will call for the grain, and will multiply it, and lay no famine upon you. And I will multiply the fruit of the tree, and the increase of the field, that ye may receive no more the reproach of famine among the nations. Then shall ye remember your evil ways, and your doings that were not good; and ye shall loathe yourselves in your own sight for your iniquities and for your abominations (36:22-31).

"Then shall ye remember!" If Israel had put into practice the promise that they made to the Lord at Sinai, when they proclaimed, "All that the LORD hath spoken we will do" (Ex 19:8), how different things would have been. They would have known the perpetual blessings of God in the land. They would have accepted the Lord Jesus Christ as their Messiah when He came the first time. They would have evaded the exile and would not have known the persecutions which the centuries have heaped upon them. But they did not. However, now at long last, in the end of time, God will demonstrate to Israel, as well as to the nations, what they could have experienced all the while, had not sin perverted the purposes of God for His people.

The prophet Zechariah depicted the coming of Israel's King-Messiah in a unique oracle in chapter 9 of his book. This prophecy pictures the judgment of God against Gentile world powers which have dominated Israel, and the subsequent Messianic kingdom which shall be established. "Behold, thy king cometh!" (v. 9) is the theme of this prophecy. But one of the interesting features of this prediction is that Zechariah presents the coming of Israel's King-Messiah in contrast to the coming of another world conqueror—Alexander the Great (vv. 1-8). Where Alexander came in great pomp, the Messiah will come in lowly circumstances, "riding upon an ass"; and yet He shall be a greater conqueror than was Alexander, for the Messiah's dominion will extend to the ends of the earth.

Ever since the days of Xerxes in the fourth century B.C., the power of the Greek city states had been on the rise and were posing an ever-increasing threat to Persia. However, it was not until Philip of Macedon succeeded in uniting them that the Hellenic League was able to deal a death blow to the Persian Empire. Philip was not the king who would realize this, however, for he was murdered in 336 B.C. It was his son, Alexander the Great, who crossed the Hellespont in 334 B.C. and forthwith routed the Persians at the battle of Grannicus. The next year he defeated Darius III at the battle of Issus in October 333 B.C., having crossed into Syria through the Cilician Gates. This opened the door to the south—Palestine and Egypt—for Alexander. It is his subsequent conquest of the cities of Syria and the Philistine plain that Zechariah presents in this prophecy which he uttered almost two centuries before it actually happened (vv. 1-7). Beginning at Hadrach and Damascus (v. 1), Alexander swept south. The Phoenician cities of Tyre and Sidon were next to fall (vv. 2-4). Tyre had held out against the Assyrians for five years. Sennacherib never did conquer it. Neither did Nebuchadnezzar, who besieged Tyre for thirteen years. But this stronghold fell to the God-given power of Alexander the Great in just seven months (cf. v. 4). Next Zechariah sees four out of the five capital cities of the Philistine plain fall to

Alexander: Ashkelon, Gaza, Ekron, and Ashdod (vv. 5-7).
After the conquest of these cities, Alexander turned toward Jerusalem to capture it. However, Zechariah sees a different fate for Jerusalem. He predicts that the city will not fall to the conqueror. "And I will encamp about my house against the army, that none pass through or return; and no oppressor shall pass through them any more: for now I have seen with mine eyes" (v. 8). Josephus tells us what happened when Alexander came against Jerusalem, and how this prediction of Zechariah was literally fulfilled two centuries after it was uttered:

> And when he [Juddus, the high priest] heard that the king was not far from the city, he went out in procession, with the priests and mass of citizens. The procession was imposing, and the manner of it different from the other nations. It reached a place called Sepha [Mt. Scopus], which word, translated into Greek, signifies a prospect, for you have thence a prospect both of Jerusalem and of the temple. Now when the Phoenicians and Chaldaeans that followed the king thought they should have liberty of plunder the city, and torture the high priest to death, which the king's displeasure made probable, the very reverse of this happened. For Alexander, when he saw the multitude at a distance in white garments, while the priests stood clothed in their fine linen, and the high priest in purple and gold robes, with his mitre on his head, and the golden plate in it whereon the name of God was engraved, he approached by himself, and adored the Name, and first saluted the high priest. The Jews also with one voice saluted Alexander, and surrounded him, whereupon the kings of Syria and the rest were astonished at what Alexander had done, and supposed him disordered in mind. However, Parmenio alone went up to him, and asked him, "How it came to pass, that when all others adored him, he should adore the high priest of the Jews?" To whom he replied, "I did not adore him, but that God who has honored him with the high priesthood. For I saw this very person in a dream in these very robes, when I was at Dium in Macedonia, who, when I was considering with myself how I might obtain the dominion of Asia, exhorted me to make no delay, but boldly to cross over, for he would conduct my army, and would give me the dominion over the Persians. And so having seen no other in such robes, and now seeing

this person in them, and remembering that vision, and the exhortation which I had in my dream, I believe that I bring this army under the divine conduct, and shall conqueror Darius, and destroy the power of the Persians, and that all things will succeed according to what is in my mind." When he had said this to Parmenio, and had given the high priest his right hand, the priests ran along by him, and he entered the city. And when he went up to the temple, he offered sacrifice to God according to the high priest's direction, and handsomely treated both the high priest and the priests. And when the book of Daniel was shown him wherein Daniel declared that one of the Greeks should destroy the empire of Persians, he supposed that he was the person meant, and full of joy dismissed the multitude for the present, but the next day called them to him, and bade them ask what favors they pleased of him.[4]

Therefore, according to Zechariah's prediction, Jerusalem was divinely protected from the destruction which Alexander might otherwise have imposed upon the city and its inhabitants. But at verse 9 the vision of the prophet now leaps into the distant future and he sees another King coming to Jerusalem. However, this time the King which he sees, in verses 9 and 10, is set in studied contrast to the splendor of Alexander. The King whom Zechariah now views is Israel's Messiah. "Rejoice greatly, O daughter of Zion; shout, O daughter of Jerusalem: behold, thy king cometh unto thee; he is just, and having salvation; lowly, and riding upon an ass, even upon a colt the foal of an ass" (v. 9). Matthew says that this prediction was also literally fulfilled during the triumphant entry of Jesus when He crossed the Mount of Olives and descended into the city of Jerusalem riding upon an ass (Mt 21:1-11).

However, Zechariah records some things which he now sees and which did not happen when Jesus entered the city of Jerusalem to the cry of the multitudes, "Hosanna to the son of David. Blessed is he that cometh in the name of the Lord; Hosanna in the highest" (Mt 21:9). The prophet says, "And I will cut off the chariot from Ephraim, and the horse from Jerusalem; and the battle bow shall be cut off; and he shall speak peace unto the nations: and his dominion shall be from sea to sea, and from the River to the ends of the earth" (Zec 9:10). It is obvious, as Matthew indicates, that verse 9 refers to the first coming of the Messiah, at which time Israel rejected her King. The great parenthesis, the age of the church, which no Old Testament prophet saw, intervenes between verses 9 and 10. Then the prophet Zechariah describes in verse 10 things which will not be fulfilled until the Messiah comes again. This is obviously the case, for universal peace did not follow the triumphant entry of Jesus into Jerusalem. He was arrested, tried, and crucified within a week of this event. In addition, within forty years the Great Revolt had brought the Romans and all the carnage which they wrought in A.D. 70. Within another half-century the Bar Kokhba revolt had failed, and the Jews were subjected to the horrible reprisals of Hadrian, only to be followed by eighteen hundred years of exile and persecution, in which the Jews were to desperately long for the very thing of which Zechariah prophesied—peace. The rabbis said, "Blessings do not in the least avail unless peace is included among them." Until this day, Israel has never known the peace which Zechariah predicted twenty-five hundred years ago. But one day she will.

If that which Zechariah predicted about Alexander's conquest of Jerusalem, two hundred years before it happened, was literally fulfilled, and if the things which Zechariah predicted about the coming of Jesus riding upon an ass to the city were literally fulfilled, five hundred years after they were predicted, then it follows that the other things which Zechariah predicted are also to find a literal fulfillment, when Jesus comes again. By what logic can the advocates of the spiritual fulfillment of Bible prophecy argue that a three-part prophecy will find a two-thirds literal fulfillment—as history has demonstrated—and then declare that the final one-third of the prophecy is to be fulfilled, not literally in Israel, but spiritually in the church? If the unprecedented behavior of Alexander the Great represented a literal fulfillment of the first third of Zechariah's prophecy, and if the triumphant entry of Jesus into Jerusalem represented a further literal fulfillment of the second third of this same prophecy, five hundred years later; then we must look for the remaining third of the prophet's prediction to be literally fulfilled even after twenty-five hundred years have passed. In addition, we must look for it to be literally fulfilled within the nation Israel, which is the prophet's frame of reference throughout.

It is in His second coming that the Lord Jesus Christ will resolve the hostility of the nations and establish His throne in Israel, from which His reign of peace will extend to the ends of the earth. The Jewish sages believed this passage from Zechariah to be Messianic. In the Talmud, Rabbi Joshua Ben-Levi asks, "It is written in one place, 'Behold, one like the Son of Man came with clouds of heaven,' but in another place it is written, 'lowly, and riding upon an ass.' How is this to be understood? The answer is, If they be righteous [or deserving] He shall come with the clouds of heaven; if they be not righteous, then He shall come lowly, and riding upon an ass." Rashi says, "This cannot be explained except of King-Messiah, for it is said of Him, 'And His dominion shall be from sea to sea'; but we do not find that such a one ruled over Israel in the time of the second Temple." Rabbi Joseph used this passage in his argument with Rabbi Hillel, who denied the coming of the Messiah, saying that He had come already during the time of Hezekiah. Said Rabbi Joseph, "Lord, forgive Rabbi Hillel! When did Hezekiah live? In the time of the first Temple. But Zechariah prophesied during the time of the second temple; 'Rejoice greatly, daughter of Zion, behold thy king cometh unto thee.'"[5]

The Jewish sages were convinced that this passage is Messianic, and though they also saw the problem involved in Messiah's coming in clouds and with great glory, and the seemingly contradictory description of His coming, lowly, and riding upon an ass, they fell short in perceiving the real truth about this passage. Though he may not have been aware of it at the time, as many of the Old Testament prophets were not fully aware of all that was involved in their prophecies, Zechariah is actually predicting the two advents of the Messiah—the Lord Jesus Christ in the humility of His first coming, and the Lord Jesus Christ in the glory of His second coming.

While Abraham was without a child, God promised that the seed of Abraham would be multiplied. "For all the land which thou seest, to thee will I give it, and to thy seed for ever. And I will make thy seed as the dust of the earth: so that if a man can number the dust of the earth, then may thy seed also be numbered" (Gen 13:15-16). "Look now toward heaven, and number the stars, if thou be able to number them: and he said unto him, So shall thy seed be" (Gen 15:5). However, when God restated the terms of the covenant just after Abraham had proved his faithfulness by taking Isaac to Mount Moriah to be offered, God said that not only would the physical seed of Abraham be numerous, but He also added that in this seed all the nations of the earth would be blessed. "I will multiply thy seed as the stars of the heavens, and as the sand which is upon the seashore; and thy seed shall possess the gate of his enemies; and in thy seed shall all nations of the earth be blessed" (Gen 22:17-28).

Does this mean all the world will be blessed because of the presence of the Jewish people, who are of the physical seed of Abraham and who stand to make a unique contribution to mankind? Perhaps. But the apostle Paul saw the real meaning of this passage, noting that the word *seed* is singular and not plural. "Now to Abraham were the promises spoken, and to his seed. He saith not, And to seeds, as of many; but as of one, And to thy seed, which is Christ" (Gal 3:16). What then is the blessing that is to be brought to all mankind through the one great Seed of Abraham, the Lord Jesus Christ? Paul tells us, "And the scripture, foreseeing that God would justify the Gentiles by faith, preached the gospel beforehand unto Abraham, saying, In thee shall all the nations be blessed" (Gal 3:8). Therefore the great Seed of Abraham is the Lord Jesus Christ, and the blessing which all nations are to receive through this Seed is that the Gentiles also should be justified by faith in Christ. But does redemption for the Gentiles, provided through the Seed of Abraham, exhaust the content of the covenant and mean that all the covenant promises of God are fulfilled spiritually in the work of the Lord Jesus, who has provided spiritual redemption for everyone—Jew and Gentile? Not at all. Centuries after God presented the blessings of the covenant to Abraham, He further elaborated the covenant by indicating that it would also include a King of the house of David upon the throne of Israel forever. The Lord said to David:

> When thy days are fulfilled, and thou shalt sleep with thy fathers, I will set up thy seed after thee, that shall proceed out of thy bowels, and I will establish his kingdom. He shall build a house for my name, and I will establish the throne of his kingdom for ever. I will be his father, and he shall be my son: if he commit iniquity, I will chasten him with the rod of men, and with the stripes of the children of men; but my loving-kindness shall not depart from him, as I took it from Saul, whom I put away before thee. And thy house and thy kingdom shall be made sure for ever before thee: thy throne shall be established for ever. According to all these words, and according to all this vision, so did Nathan speak unto David (2 Sa 7:12-17).

This promise was reconfirmed many times during the subsequent history of Israel:

> In that day will I raise up the tabernacle of David that is fallen, and close up the breaches thereof; and I will raise up its ruins, and I will build it as in the days of old (Amos 9:11).

> For unto us a child is born, unto us a son is given; and the government shall be upon his shoulder: and his name shall be called Wonderful, Counsellor, Mighty God, Everlasting Father, Prince of Peace. Of the increase of his government and of peace there shall be no end, upon the throne of David, and upon his kingdom, to establish it, and to uphold it with justice and with righteousness from henceforth even for ever. The zeal of the LORD of hosts will perform this (Is 9:6-7).

> Behold, the days come, saith the LORD, that I will raise unto David a righteous Branch, and he shall reign as king and deal wisely, and shall execute justice and righteousness in the land. In his days Judah shall be saved, and Israel shall dwell safely; and this is his name whereby he shall be called: the LORD our righteousness (Jer 23:5-6).

> And it shall come to pass in that day, saith the LORD of hosts, that I will break his yoke from off thy neck, and will burst

thy bonds; and strangers shall no more make him their bond-man; but they shall serve the LORD their God, and David their king, whom I will raise up unto them (Jer 30:8-9).

And my servant David shall be king over them; and they all shall have one shepherd: they shall also walk in mine ordinances, and observe my statutes, and do them. And they shall dwell in the land that I have given unto Jacob my servant, wherein your fathers dwelt; and they shall dwell therein, they, and their children, and their children's children, for ever: and David my servant shall be their prince for ever (Eze 37:24-25).

But my lovingkindness will I not utterly take from him, Nor suffer my faithfulness to fail. My covenant will I not break, Nor alter the thing that is gone out of my lips. Once have I sworn by my holiness: I will not lie unto David: His seed shall endure for ever, And his throne as the sun before me. It shall be established for ever as the moon, And as the faithful witness in the sky (Ps 89:33-37).

All of these Scriptures found their fulfillment in the Lord Jesus Christ, according to Luke:

And the angel said unto her, Fear not, Mary: for thou hast found favor with God. And behold, thou shalt conceive in thy womb, and bring forth a son, and shalt call his name JESUS. He shall be great, and shall be called the Son of the Most High: and the Lord God shall give unto him the throne of his father David: and he shall reign over the house of Jacob for ever; and of his kingdom there shall be no end. And Mary said unto the angel, How shall this be, seeing I know not a man? And the angel answered and said unto her, The Holy Spirit shall come upon thee, and the power of the Most High shall overshadow thee: wherefore also the holy thing which is begotten shall be called the Son of God (Lk 1:30-35).

Though all Christian expositors agree that these regal promises found their fulfillment in the Lord Jesus Christ, the greater Son of David, there is difference of opinion concerning just how they are fulfilled. Many assume that these kingdom promises made to Israel are to be spiritualized and reapplied to the church, which became spiritual Israel when the nation Israel rejected the Lord Jesus Christ as Messiah and had Him nailed to a cross.

However, the Bible teaches four great truths about the coming of the kingdom of God. First, a literal kingdom is promised in the Old Testament. Second, the kingdom is offered to Israel in the gospels (Mt 3:1-2; 4:17; 10:5-7). Third, when Israel rejected the kingdom by rejecting the King, the kingdom was postponed as far as the nation Israel is concerned (Mt 23:37-39). However, though Israel rejected her King and the kingdom that He offered, the kingdom did not disappear from the earth, for the Lord Jesus Christ now reigns as King in each born-again believer. "And being asked by the Pharisees, when the kingdom of God cometh, he answered them and said, The kingdom of God cometh not with observation: neither shall they say, Lo, here! or, There! for lo, the kingdom of God is within you" (Lk 17:20-21). But these facts concerning the kingdom do not exhaust its content. The kingdom has eschatological dimensions which as yet are unrealized. Therefore, in the fourth place, the kingdom will be finally realized in the nation Israel at the second coming of Christ. This is why Jesus spoke as He did, saying to His disciples, "But ye are they that have continued with me in my temptation; and I appoint unto you a kingdom, even as my Father appointed unto me, that ye may eat and drink at my table in my kingdom; and ye shall sit on thrones judging the twelve tribes of Israel" (Lk 22:28-30). "And Jesus said unto them, Verily I say unto you, that ye who have followed me, in the regeneration when the Son of man shall sit on the throne of his glory, ye also shall sit upon twelve thrones, judging the twelve tribes of Israel" (Mt 19:28). This is also the reason why Jesus did not categorically reject the idea of a future literal kingdom in Israel when His disciples asked him the question, "Lord, dost thou at this time restore the kingdom to Israel?" (Ac 1:6). His answer indicates the postponement of the kingdom rather than the elimination of it. "And he said unto them, It is not for you to know times or seasons, which the Father hath set within his own authority" (v. 7; cf. 3:19-21).

On October 13, 1971, the following story appeared in *The Jerusalem Post*:

> Tel Aviv—Mr. David Ben-Gurion, 83 years and one day old, told a gathering of new immigrants at the closing ceremony of the Aliyada here on Thursday that one of the chief tasks facing Israel in the coming decade is to increase the Jewish population to 6,000,000. Mr. Ben-Gurion, who was the guest of the Association of Americans and Canadians on the occasion of his birthday, was received enthusiastically as he entered the amphitheatre at the Exhibition Grounds. Some of the immigrants began to sing, "David King of Israel is alive!"

This is sheer idealism. However, it indicates that the *ideal* is still alive in the minds of the people of Israel. Though there has not been a Davidic king on the throne of Israel since the first exile, twenty-five hundred years ago, the aspiration lingers still. And that for a very good reason. The Jewish Scriptures declare that the throne of David would not be obviated in the course of history, but that in the last days it will be found intact. If the people of Israel disobeyed the terms of the Sinai covenant, they would be punished with exile, and the throne of David would fail (1 Ki 8:21-26); but this demise of the throne would not be a permanent consequence of disobedience, nor would the promise be diverted into categories of spiritual fulfillment. After the punishment of the exile, the throne would again be established.

How has this theme worked itself out in the history of Israel?

The last king of the house of David to reign in Judah was King Zedekiah. Nebuchadnezzar placed him upon the throne during the first years of the Babylonian dominion of Judah. He reigned for eleven years, but his reign came to an end with an ill-advised and ill-fated rebellion against Nebuchadnezzar. Attempting to escape Jerusalem Zedekiah was captured and blinded—the last sight that he saw was that of his children being put to death before his eyes. Zedekiah was taken to Babylon, where he died many years later. From that day until this, there has not been a king of the house of David upon the throne of Israel. There were other kings to reign in Judah after the exile. However, these were Hasmoneans, descendants of the priestly family of Modin, who instigated the Maccabeean revolt against Antiochus IV Epiphanes and the Seleucid dominion in Judah. At first these Hasmoneans served as priestly leaders of the nation. However, during the reign of John Hyrcanus (134-104 B.C.) these priests began to look upon themselves as sovereign rulers. It was Hyrcanus' son, Aristobulus, (103 B.C.) who actually took to himself the title of king. The Hasmonean dynasty lapsed into decay and finally died out when Mariamne, as Hasmonean, married Herod the Great (37-4 B.C.) of the royal house of Idumea.

It was the belief in the eternity of the house of David (1 Mac 2:57) which kept the Hasmonean dynasty from complete acceptance and which predicated for them a reign only until the true prophet arose. The Apocrypha says, "Also that the Jews and priests were well pleased that Simon [a Hasmonean] should be their governor and high priest forever, until there should arise a faithful prophet" (1 Mac 14:41). Many believed that the Hasmonean house would eventually give way to the house of David.

The idea of a king in the line of David never died out. Even after the Great Revolt in A.D. 70 the idea of a king who would be the Son of David was considered so much a Messianic prerequisite that the Roman emperors Vespasian, Domitian, and Trajan ordered that any Jew who claimed to be of the house of David should be killed.

Obviously there was no king of the house of David upon the throne of Israel during the long centuries of the second exile, as there is none today, even though the State of Israel exists again.

David was anointed king of Israel long before the nation recognized him as such. It was during the reign of King Saul that God instructed Samuel to seek out David and anoint him. He was still a lad tending his father's sheep in Bethlehem (1 Sa 16:1-12). Though David was anointed king at that time, he did not claim the throne for many years to come. It was not until Saul was killed at the battle of Mount Gilboa that the men of Judah then proclaimed David as king (2 Sa 2:1-7), and it was not for some time after that that all Israel recognized him as king. "David was thirty years old when he began to reign, and he reigned forty years. In

Hebron he reigned over Judah seven years and six months; and in Jerusalem he reigned thirty and three years over all Israel and Judah" (2 Sa 5:4-5).

Just as David was anointed king of Israel and then much time elapsed before he claimed the throne, so the Lord Jesus Christ, the greater Son of David, the anointed King of Israel, is yet unrecognized by His own people. However, He too, after a delay of many centuries, will one day claim the throne. The prophet Hosea saw this delay and said,

> For the children of Israel shall abide many days without king, and without prince, and without sacrifice, and without pillar, and without ephod or teraphim: afterward shall the children of Israel return, and seek the LORD their God, and David their king, and shall come with fear unto the LORD and to his goodness in the latter days (Ho 3:4-5).

When will this be? The prophet Jeremiah indicates that there are two things which will usher in the reign of Messiah-King. The first is the time of tribulation that is yet to come:

> And these are the words that the LORD spake concerning Israel and concerning Judah. For thus saith the LORD: We have heard a voice of trembling, of fear, and not of peace. Ask ye now, and see whether a man doth travail with child: wherefore do I see every man with his hands on his loins, as a woman in travail, and all faces are turned into paleness? Alas! for that day is great, so that none is like it: it is even the time of Jacob's trouble; but he shall be saved out of it. And it shall come to pass in that day, saith the LORD of hosts, that I will break his yoke from off thy neck, and will burst thy bonds; and strangers shall no more make him their bondman; but they shall serve the LORD their God, and David their king, whom I will raise up unto them. Therefore fear thou not, O Jacob my servant, saith the LORD; neither be dismayed, O Israel: for, lo, I will save thee from afar, and thy seed from the land of their captivity; and Jacob shall return, and shall be quiet and at ease, and none shall make him afraid. For I am with thee, saith the LORD, to save thee: for I will make a full end of all the nations whither I have scattered thee, but I will not make a full end of thee; but I will correct

thee in measure, and will in no wise leave thee unpunished (Jer 30:4-11).

The second is the restoration of the nation Israel:

> Behold, the days come, saith the LORD, that I will perform that good word which I have spoken concerning the house of Israel and concerning the house of Judah. In those days, and at that time, will I cause a Branch of righteousness to grow up unto David; and he shall execute justice and righteousness in the land. In those days shall Judah be saved, and Jerusalem shall dwell safely; and this is the name whereby she shall be called: the LORD our righteousness. For thus saith the LORD: David shall never want a man to sit upon the throne of the house of Israel (Jer 33:14-17).

Jesus combines these two elements in His prophetic discourse:

> But immediately after the tribulation of those days the sun shall be darkened, and the moon shall not give her light, and the stars shall fall from heaven, and the powers of the heavens shall be shaken: and then shall appear the sign of the Son of man in heaven: and then shall all the tribes of the earth mourn, and they shall see the Son of man coming on the clouds of heaven with power and great glory. And he shall send forth his angels with a great sound of a trumpet, and they shall gather together his elect from the four winds, from one end of heaven to the other (Mt 24:29-31).

After the great tribulation period has prepared Israel to yearn for the Messiah, the Lord Jesus Christ will return to the earth again. The nation Israel, whose forefathers cried, "Not this man, but Barabbas" (Jn 18:40), will, in effect, cry on that day, "Not Barabbas, but this man!" When Israel receives the Branch whom the Lord has raised in the house of David, her iniquity will be removed, for "In that day there shall be a fountain opened to the house of David and to the inhabitants of Jerusalem, for sin and for uncleanness" (Zec 13:1). And it shall occur at that moment when the Lord Jesus returns. "For, behold, I will bring forth my servant the Branch. . . .And I will remove the iniquity of that land in one day" (Zec 3:8-9).

Not only will Israel's iniquity be cleansed in that day, but a great spiritual transformation is to take place. This event is the new covenant phase of the original covenant. It has to do with the granting of a new heart to the remnant of the covenant people who survive the great tribulation period and witness the second coming of Christ.

Joseph Klausner has written,

> In the course of the long evolution of the Jewish Messianic idea, two different conceptions were inseparably woven together: politico-national salvation and religio-spiritual redemption. These two elements walked arm in arm. The Messiah must be both king and redeemer. He must overthrow the enemies of Israel, establish the kingdom of Israel, and rebuild the Temple; and at the same time he must reform the world through the Kingdom of God, root out idolatry from the world, proclaim the one and only God to all, put an end to sin, and be wise, pious, and just as no man had been before him or ever would be after him. In short, he is the great political and spiritual hero at one and the same time. 'My kingdom is not of this world!'—this saying attributed to Jesus by the Gospel of John (18:36), cannot be imagined in the mouth of a Jewish Messiah, not even a Messiah of the more spiritual type portrayed in the Psalms of Solomon.[6]

Klausner is a Jew and fails to understand the teachings of Jesus about the interim nature of the kingdom which is within the believer during the great parenthesis, the age of the church. But he does insist that the Messianic hope has both a political and a spiritual content. This is consistent with the teachings of all the Scripture, for both the Old Testament and the New Testament affirm that the Lord Jesus Christ, Israel's Messiah, will reign upon the throne of David in a literal kingdom on earth, but that He will also spiritually regenerate His people Israel.

To say that this coming spiritual transformation of the nation Israel is the new covenant does not obviate the fact that Christians are also partakers of this new covenant. They are. This is made manifest and substantiated each time a local church gathers to observe the Lord's Supper. Paul says:

> For I received of the Lord that which also I delivered unto you, that the Lord Jesus in the night in which he was betrayed took bread; and when he had given thanks, he brake it, and said, This is my body, which is for you: this do in remembrance of me. In like manner also the cup, after supper, saying, This cup is the new covenant in my blood: this do, as often as ye drink it, in remembrance of me (1 Co 11:23-25).

The writer of the book of Hebrews also indicates this, for he declares that the Christian in this age has already experienced the essence of the new covenant, mediated to him personally by the work of the Lord Jesus Christ (Heb 8, 10). This indicates that the spiritual transformation which the remnant in Israel will experience after the great tribulation is concluded is not unlike that spiritual transformation which the believer has already experienced in this age.

Many scholars see Christianity as the fulfillment of the highest aspirations of Judaism. Hence, Judaism is left unfulfilled and exhausted. This depletion, via fulfillment, leaves the Jews on a dead-end street. While it is true that the spiritual aspirations of the Old Testament find their highest fulfillment in the gospel of Jesus Christ, it is not true that the gospel fulfills and thereby annuls the original covenant made with Israel. The Sinai covenant, with its conditional requirements for blessing, did not annul the unconditional Abrahamic covenant, says Paul (Gal 3:17-18). Neither does the preaching of the gospel in this age set aside forever the covenant promises of God made to the nation Israel. They were unconditionally given: they will be unconditionally fulfilled. Though Gentile believers during this, the church age, are beneficiaries of the blessings of the new covenant, the remnant representatives of Israel nationally will also experience these blessings when Jesus comes again. Two basic passages in the prophets affirm this.

The first major passage is found in Jeremiah 31:31-37. During the days just prior to the first exile, Jeremiah proclaims that God is not finished with the nation Israel. There is yet in store for the covenant people a great spiritual transformation:

> Behold, the days come, saith the LORD, that I will make a

new covenant with the house of Israel, and with the house of Judah: not according to the covenant that I made with their fathers in the day that I took them by the hand to bring them out of the land of Egypt; which my covenant they brake, although I was a husband unto them, saith the LORD. But this is the covenant that I will make with the house of Israel after those days, saith the LORD: I will put my law in their inward parts, and in their heart will I write it; and I will be their God, and they shall be my people: and they shall teach no more every man his neighbor, and every man his brother, saying, Know the LORD; for they shall all know me, from the least of them unto the greatest of them, saith the LORD: for I will forgive their iniquity, and their sin will I remember no more (Jer 31:31-34).

Paul says that this will be fulfilled when "all Israel shall be saved" *after* the "fulness of the Gentiles be come in," and Israel's "hardening in part" be removed. He also tells us when to expect this fulfillment—when "there shall come out of Zion the Deliverer" (Ro 11:25-27). This locates the time of this great spiritual transformation. It will occur, Paul says, only after the mystery age of the church has run its course and God's work with the Gentiles, in which He has called out from among them a people for His name, is completed (Ac 15:14-18). During this time the nation Israel is spiritually blinded. But the veil will be lifted when Jesus comes, and the remnant of Israel which survives the great tribulation will then experience this incomparable spiritual awakening.

Ezekiel, who prophesied during the first exile, promised essentially the same thing:

And I will sprinkle clean water upon you, and ye shall be clean: from all your filthiness, and from all your idols, will I cleanse you. A new heart also will I give you, and a new spirit will I put within you; and I will take away the stony heart out of your flesh, and I will give you a heart of flesh. And I will put my Spirit within you, and cause you to walk in my statutes, and ye shall keep mine ordinances, and do them. And ye shall dwell in the land that I gave to your fathers; and ye shall be my people, and I will be your God. And I will save you from all your uncleannesses: and I will call for the grain, and will multiply it, and lay no famine upon you. And I will multiply the fruit of the tree, and the increase of the field, that ye may receive no more the reproach of famine among the nations. Then shall ye remember your evil ways, and your doings that were not good; and ye shall loathe yourselves in your own sight for your iniquities and for your abominations (Eze 36:25-31).

The apostle Paul locates the time of this event in terms of the completion of the mystery age of the church, declaring that Israel's spiritual transformation will occur only after the great parenthesis has enabled the body of Christ to form. But these two prophets, Jeremiah and Ezekiel, also locate the time of this event, for they both affirm that it will occur only after Israel has been regathered back to the land. Jeremiah says:

> For thus saith the LORD, Sing with gladness for Jacob, and shout for the chief of the nations: publish ye, praise ye, and say, O LORD, save they people, the remnant of Israel. Behold, I will bring them from the north country, and gather them from the uttermost parts of the earth, and with them the blind and the lame, the woman with child and her that travaileth with child together: a great company shall they return hither. . . .Hear the word of the LORD, O ye nations, and declare it in the isles afar off; and say, He that scattered Israel will gather him, and keep him, as a shepherd doth his flock. For the LORD hath ransomed Jacob, and redeemed him from the hand of him that was stronger than he. . . .Thus saith the LORD: Refrain thy voice from weeping, and thine eyes from tears; for thy work shall be rewarded, saith the LORD; and they shall come again from the land of the enemy (Jer 31:7-8; 10-11; 16).

Ezekiel also prefaces his prediction about the new heart and the new spirit by declaring, "For I will take you from among the nations, and gather you out of all the countries, and will bring you into your own land" (36:24). Since it is obvious that this spiritual transformation did not take place after the return from the first exile, it must be left for a future fulfillment, sometime after the current return from the second exile.

It is significant that the new covenant is presented not so much as a part of the Abrahamic covenant, but in contrast to the Sinai covenant (Jer 31:32). Because the terms of the new covenant are unconditional in nature, this relates it to the Abrahamic covenant. But it is contrasted with the Sinai covenant for the same reason. It is God's answer to the failure of Israel. Under the conditional terms of the Sinai covenant, Israel was to be blessed if she remained faithful to the commandments. But all ended in failure, for this was precisely what Israel was unable to do. The judgment of the exile—Israel's unique punishment for failure under the terms of the Sinai covenant—followed.

There are three words which characterize the Sinai covenant in contrast to the new covenant. The Sinai covenant was *static*, *external*, and *negative*. The key to Israel's failure to keep the Sinai covenant and the subsequent exile is also found in these three words.

First, the Sinai covenant was *static*. It made requirements, but its only dynamic was the vague promise of blessings for conformity and punishment for nonconformity. As a sufficient incentive these could impart neither the *desire* nor the *power* to keep the law. To offset this, the new covenant will impart to Israel both a new heart and a new spirit. In the new heart, a new desire will be granted. In the new spirit a new power will be imparted. This, Paul says, God has already done for the believer in this age, "For it is God who worketh in you both to will [desire] and to work [power], for his good pleasure" (Phil 2:13).

It is because the born-again believer during this present age has received a new heart (2 Co 5:17) and is indwelt by the Holy Spirit (Ro 8:9-11) that the believer is also a participant in the new covenant (Heb 10:12-18). However, its original intended recipient is Israel. And the ultimate recipients of its dynamic will be Israel. When Jesus comes again and the remnant in Israel which survives the great tribulation period receives Him as Messiah, this spiritual transformation will occur. The covenant people will be born again. They will receive a new heart. In addition, the Holy Spirit, who today indwells the church, will be poured out upon Israel in those days:

> And they shall know that I am the LORD their God, in that I
> caused them to go into captivity among the nations, and have
> gathered them unto their own land; and I will leave none of
> them any more there; neither will I hide my face any more
> from them; for I have poured out my Spirit upon the house of
> Israel, saith the Lord GOD (Eze 39:28-29).

> For I will pour water upon him that is thirsty, and streams
> upon the dry ground; I will pour my Spirit upon thy seed, and
> my blessing upon thine offspring. . . .And a Redeemer will
> come to Zion, and unto them that turn from transgression in
> Jacob, saith the LORD. And as for me, this is my covenant
> with them, saith the LORD: my Spirit that is upon thee, and
> my words which I have put in thy mouth, shall not depart out
> of thy mouth, nor out of the mouth of thy seed's seed, saith
> the Lord, from henceforth and for ever (Is 44:3; 59:20-21).

Second, the Sinai covenant was *external*. It was characterized by a series of laws being imposed from without upon
the people. Moses carried the terms of the Sinai covenant
written upon tablets of stone down from the mountain. But in
contrast, the new covenant will be written upon the heart. It
will be inward. "And I will give them one heart, and I will put
a new spirit within you; and I will take the stony heart out of
their flesh, and will give them a heart of flesh; that they may
walk in my statutes, and keep mine ordinances, and do them:
and they shall be my people, and I will be their God" (Eze
11:19-20). Israel will walk in the Lord's statutes due to an
inward desire to do so, just as the believer during this present
age has an inward desire to serve Jesus and to walk in His
commandments.

Third, the Sinai covenant was *negative*. It was written
largely in terms of "thou shalt not." In contrast, the new
covenant will be positive, written in terms of what Israel will
want to do through the impetus of this new spiritual
dynamic. No longer will Israel need the meticulous regulations of the Talmud to hedge in the law and regulate obedience to it. The covenant people will obey through the positive impetus of love (cf. Ro 8:8-10; Gal 5:14).

Why did God mark out Israel for this particular spiritual
destiny? Ezekiel concludes his prediction about the new

covenant with these words of explanation about God's choice of Israel:

> Not for your sake do I this, saith the Lord GOD, be it known unto you: be ashamed and confounded for your ways, O house of Israel. Thus saith the Lord GOD: In the day that I cleanse you from all your iniquities, I will cause the cities to be inhabited, and the waste places shall be builded. And the land that was desolate shall be tilled, whereas it was a desolation in the sight of all that passed by. And they shall say, This land that was desolate is become like the garden of Eden; and the waste and desolate and ruined cities are fortified and inhabited. Then the nations that are left round about you shall know that I, the LORD, have builded the ruined places, and planted that which was desolate: I, the LORD, have spoken it, and I will do it (36:32-36).

Therefore, throughout the millennial earth, redeemed Israel will bear witness to the nations concerning what God can do to, and by, and in, and for, and through a people who are uniquely His own. Of course, Israel could have experienced this long ago if their forefathers had yielded to the Messiah when He came the first time. They did not. But their rejection did not annul the covenant intentions of God to glorify His own name by blessing Israel (Eze 36:22-23). God will yet accomplish in the Lord's second coming what Israel forfeited the first time Jesus came.

A woman came one day to Rabbi Israel, who was a disciple of the great Baal Shem-Tob, founder of the Hasidic movement, and complained to him that her husband had ceased to love her. "When we married he loved me dearly, but now his affection has turned away from me." Rabbi Israel lifted up his hands and exclaimed, "I have the same complaint against Thee, O Lord. When Thou didst choose Israel to be Thy bride at Sinai, Thou didst truly love her. Be not unto us as this woman's spouse unto her, but show us again Thy love and redeem us."

And so He shall!

The nation Israel is not the only beneficiary of the Messianic kingdom of the Son of David. The Messiah's reign in

Israel will be the frame of reference for a vast world dominion of peace and prosperity which will affect all men.

First, the Messianic kingdom will include the faithful
remnant in Israel which survives the great tribulation period
and which is spiritually regenerated, having repented and
received the Lord Jesus Christ as Saviour and Messiah
at His second coming. The rabbis debated whether the
Messiah's reign would include the ten tribes, or just Judah.
Rabbi Akiba said, "The Ten Tribes shall not return again,
for it is written, (Deu 29:28) 'and the LORD rooted them out
of their land in anger, and in wrath, and in great indignation,
and cast them into another land, as at this day.' As 'this day'
goes and returns not, so do they go and return not."

Rabbi Akiba's attitude toward the ten tribes may have
been due to his disappointment with the dispersed Jews
among whom he had journeyed in an attempt to stir up
rebellion against the Roman Empire at the time of the Bar
Kokhba revolt. They were reluctant to join the fight, and this
lack of nationalism led Rabbi Akiba to this harsh judgment.
However, there is ample evidence that the faithful remnant
which returns to form the nucleus of the Messianic kingdom
will include both Judah and Israel.

In Ezekiel's vision of the valley of dry bones, in which the
Lord predicts that the nation will live again, the Lord also
instructs Ezekiel to bind two sticks together so that the
people will know, when he explains the meaning of his
action, that both Israel and Judah have a part in the Messianic kingdom. He then concludes by saying:

> And the sticks whereon thou writest shall be in thy hand
> before their eyes. And say unto them, Thus saith the Lord
> GOD: Behold, I will take the children of Israel from among
> the nations, whither they are gone, and will gather them on
> every side, and bring them into their own land: and I will
> make them one nation in the land, upon the mountains of
> Israel; and one king shall be king to them all; and they shall be
> no more two nations, neither shall they be divided into two
> kingdoms any more at all; neither shall they defile themselves
> any more with their idols, nor with their detestable things,
> nor with any of their transgressions; but I will save them out
> of all their dwelling-places, wherein they have sinned, and

will cleanse them: so shall they be my people, and I will be their God. And my servant David shall be king over them; and they all shall have one shepherd: they shall also walk in mine ordinances, and observe my statutes, and do them. And they shall dwell in the land that I have given unto Jacob my servant, wherein your fathers dwelt; and they shall dwell therein, they, and their children, and their children's children, for ever: and David my servant shall be their prince for ever. Moreover I will make a covenant of peace with them; it shall be an everlasting covenant with them; and I will place them, and multiply them, and will set my sanctuary in the midst of them for evermore. My tabernacle also shall be with them; and I will be their God, and they shall be my people. And the nations shall know that I am the LORD that sanctifieth Israel, when my sanctuary shall be in the midst of them for evermore (Eze 37:20-28).

The Official Associated Press Almanac for 1974 estimates the total population of world Jewry at about 13,989,650. Over two and one-half million of these now live in Israel during these closing days of the second exile. Others will be gathered out of the diaspora at the second coming of Christ. This will complete the regathering which was promised by the prophets. However, the total population of world Jewry seems to be greatly reduced during the great tribulation period as a result of the persecutions by the Antichrist. Therefore the remnant of living Jews who go into the Messianic kingdom will not be large. But for that matter, the remnant which returned from the first exile to reconstitute the nation was not large either. Ezekiel predicted this in one of the pantomimes which the Lord instructed him to perform (Eze 5:1-12). He was to take a sword as sharp as a barber's razor and cut some hair from his head and beard. This hair was to be parted into three groups. One group was to be burnt with fire—representing those Jews who would be killed at the siege of Jerusalem in 587 B.C. Another group was to be scattered to the wind—representing the exiles who would disappear. Then he was instructed to "take thereof a few in number, and bind them in thy skirts" (v. 3). These few represent the remnant which would return from the Babylonian exile. Isaiah says the same thing:

> And it shall come to pass in that day, that the remnant of
> Israel, and they that are escaped of the house of Jacob, shall
> no more again lean upon him that smote them, but shall lean
> upon the LORD, the Holy One of Israel, in truth. A rem-
> nant shall return, even the remnant of Jacob, unto the
> mighty God. For though thy people, Israel, be as the sand of
> the sea, only a remnant of them shall return: a destruction is
> determined, over-flowing with righteousness. For a full end,
> and that determined, will the Lord, the GOD of hosts, make in
> the midst of all the earth (10:20-23).

But, just as a few in number—a faithful remnant—returned
from the first exile, so a comparatively few will constitute
the faithful remnant of returned exiles who survive the tribulation period and enter into the Messianic kingdom (Is
11:11-16).

Will there be Gentile subjects in the Messianic kingdom?
The rabbis generally agreed that all Gentiles, except the
Romans, would have their part in the golden age. An ancient
legend says:

> In the Tabernacle, as later in the Temple, gold, silver and
> brass were employed, but not iron. God meant to indicate by
> the exclusion of iron that "in the future time the golden
> Babylon, the silver Media, and the brazen Greece," would
> be permitted to bestow gifts on the new Temple, but not "the
> iron of Rome." It is true that Babylon also destroyed the
> sanctuary of God, like Rome, but not with such fury and such
> thorough-going wrath as Rome, whose sons cried: "Raze it,
> raze it, even to the foundations thereof," and for this reason
> Rome may not contribute to the Messianic Temple. But as
> God will reject the gifts of Rome, so also will the Messiah, to
> whom all the nations of the earth will have to offer gifts.
> Egypt will come with her gifts, and although the Messiah will
> at first refuse to accept anything from the former taskmaster
> of Israel, God will say to him: "The Egyptians granted My
> children an abode in their land, do not repulse them." Then
> the Messiah will accept their gift. After Egypt will follow her
> neighbour, Ethiopia, with her gifts, thinking that if the Mes-
> siah accepted gifts from the former taskmaster of Israel, he
> will also accept gifts from her. Then the Messiah will also
> accept others with their gifts, and all will be accepted—save
> those from Rome.[7]

THE COMING OF ISRAEL'S MESSIAH

In contrast to the reluctance expressed in this legend, the prophets of Israel indicated that the nations would be a part of the Messianic kingdom:

> And it shall come to pass in the latter days, that the mountain of the LORD's house shall be established on the top of the mountains, and shall be exalted above the hills; and all nations shall flow unto it. And many peoples shall go and say, Come ye, and let us go up to the mountain of the LORD, to the house of the God of Jacob; and he will teach us of his ways, and we will walk in his paths: for out of Zion shall go forth the law, and the word of the LORD from Jerusalem (Is 2:2-4; cf. 19:18-24).

Jesus also indicated the Gentile position in the Messianic kingdom (Mt 8:11).

Besides the redeemed Jews and Gentiles who survive the great tribulation period to enter the Messianic kingdom, it will also be composed of the church, the Old Testament saints, and the martyred tribulation saints. All of these will be faithful and loyal subjects of the Messianic kingdom on earth. All of these have resurrection bodies as well as redeemed souls, and therefore they are incapable of sin. However, their having resurrection bodies also renders them incapable of reproduction (cf. Mt 22:28-30).

At this point we are faced with one of the crucial questions of the whole millennial concept: Will there actually be an environment at the end of time when, for a while, the earth will be inhabited by two groups of people—one group having natural bodies, the other having resurrection bodies? This seems to be one of the greatest contentions in the amillennial opposition to the view of a literal reign of the Messiah upon the earth. All else in the premillennial interpretation may be feasible save this. Many sincere amillennial Christians just cannot abide this teaching. However, the answer to the proposition is *yes*; the prophetic Word does indicate that this is the case. But the radical nature of the issue is eased when we remember that there have been periods in past time when something akin to this has occurred on earth. At the beginning of time, for example, we have this strange text in Genesis:

> And it came to pass, when men began to multiply on the face of the ground, and daughters were born unto them, that the sons of God saw the daughters of men that they were fair; and they took them wives of all that they chose. And the LORD said, My Spirit shall not strive with man forever, for that he also is flesh: yet shall his days be a hundred and twenty years. The Nephilim were in the earth in those days, and also after that, when the sons of God came in unto the daughters of men, and they bare children to them: the same were the mighty men that were of old, the men of renown (Gen 6:1-4).

Many believe that fallen angels cohabited with mortal women and produced a hybrid, part natural and part supernatural, people called Nephilim. If this be the case, then these fallen angels must have inhabited human male bodies to accomplish this, because the angels are sexless.[8] It is for this reason that the curse mentioned in 2 Peter 2:4 and Jude 6 was placed upon these angels. The flood was necessary, among other reasons, to wipe this race off the earth. Whatever one's interpretation of this mysterious passage, it suggests that in the antediluvian world the population could have been composed of both natural and supernatural people. Also, we might remember that when Jesus died upon the cross a mysterious pehnomenon occurred which introduced resurrected bodies into the natural environment for a while (cf Mt 27:52-53). These parallels, if not complete in their analogy, do offer some precedence for the idea of both natural and supernatural bodies inhabiting the earth at the same time. After all, the Lord Jesus Christ Himself mingled freely with His disciples when He had been raised from the dead. His resurrection body did not preclude the possibility of social intercourse with people who were yet in their natural bodies.

The first group of those who will be subjects of the Messianic reign of Christ upon the earth and who will have resurrection bodies, is the church. Though the church in the New Testament is presented as a local and visible congregation of born-again, baptized believers, the New Testament also calls the body of Christ, composed of all born-again believers in every age, the church (cf. Eph 1:22-23). The history of the church on earth is bounded by Pentecost, when it began, and by the rapture, when the church will be taken out of the world. The church age is a great parenthesis injected between God's dealing with the nation Israel, which was suspended at the cross and will be resumed again during the tribulation period. The age of the church began with spiritual resurrection for all who would repent and believe the gospel. It will end in physical resurrection for all those, Jew and Gentile, who have believed on the Lord Jesus Christ and have been saved. This physical resurrection will occur when Jesus returns for His own and they, the church, are caught up to meet Him in the air (1 Th 4:13-16). That generation of born-again believers who are alive when Jesus comes will also be caught up to meet Him (1 Co 15:52; 1 Th 4:17). The dead believers will receive resurrection bodies, as will that generation of living believers (Phil 3:21; 1 Jn 3:2).

In the tribulation period, the church will be with Christ, where the judgment seat is set and rewards are distributed to every believer (2 Co 5:10-11). At the second coming of Christ, which brings to a close the great tribulation period on earth, the church will return to the earth with Him (Col 3:4; Rev 19:14). Every believer who makes up the church will then inhabit the earth during the Messianic age.

The second group of those who will inhabit the millennial earth and who will have resurrection bodies is composed of both the Old Testament saints and the tribulation martyrs.

The Old Testament saints are not raised from the dead at the rapture of the church. Only the dead in Christ will rise at the rapture (1 Th 4:16). This is why Paul calls this resurrection a mystery (1 Co 15:51). The fact of bodily resurrection was no mystery. It was taught in several passages in the Old Testament. What constituted the mystery is the newly revealed truth that the church would experience a resurrection, separate and unique, from that which would be experienced by the Old Testament saints. Daniel 12:2 speaks of a resurrection which occurs immediately after the great tribulation period is over. It is then that the Old Testament saints who, like Abraham, have been justified by faith, will be raised from the dead. Apparently those, both Jews and Gentiles, who are saved during the tribulation period and who die for their commitment to Christ, will also be raised at this time. Though no specific Scripture supports this supposition, it is a reasonable conjecture, for these tribulation martyrs are seen around the throne in Revelation 7:13-17.

Therefore the subjects of the Messianic reign are not the homogeneous group of resurrected saints which will eternally populate heaven. The Messianic age is a part of history rather than eternity. It is not heaven. Heaven is the ultimate state of the redeemed. Heaven awaits the purging of the earth by fire (2 Pe 3:10-13), and the descent of the New Jerusalem (Rev 21-22). In contrast to the homogeneous eternal state of the redeemed, is the heterogeneous group which will make up the subjects of the Messianic age. Some, like the survivors of the great tribulation period, will have natural bodies. Others, such as the church, the Old Testament saints, and the tribulation martyrs, will have resurrection bodies. As the Messianic age progresses, generations of unregenerated sinners will emerge and will contest the Messiah's reign. They will be kept in subjection by His rod of iron (Ps 2:9; 110:1-7). It is this dissident group whom Satan will finally lead in revolt against the Messiah at the close of the period. However, this rebellion will be futile, and when it is put down, rebellion against God will be forever banished from the universe:

> And when the thousand years are finished, Satan shall be loosed out of his prison, and shall come forth to deceive the nations which are in the four corners of the earth, Gog and Magog, to gather them together to the war: the number of whom is as the sand of the sea. And they went up over the breadth of the earth, and compassed the camp of the saints about, and the beloved city: and fire came down out of heaven and devoured them. And the devil that deceived them was cast into the lake of fire and brimstone, where are also the beast and the false prophet; and they shall be tormented day and night for ever and ever (Rev 20:7-10).

Jerusalem was selected by David as the capital of the kingdom of Israel when he left Hebron, where he had reigned as king over Judah. Solomon gave it its greatest glory. A generation later it became the provincial capital of

Judah. After the exile, Jerusalem was the focal point of the Jewish faith and the administrative capital of the Persians, as well as of the Greek Ptolemys and the Seleucids. When the Maccabean revolt had, for a time, freed Jerusalem of Gentile dominion, it contained the palace of the Hasmonean dynasty. Later, after the conquest of Pompey, Jerusalem was the throne city during the Roman reign of Herod the Great. However, the Roman governors who followed Herod administered the Judean province from Caesarea. Then for the next two thousand years, from the time of Herod until the new State of Israel established its parliament there, the city of Jerusalem enjoyed capital status only briefly during the Crusades when the capital of the Frankish kingdom of Jerusalem was established there between 1099 and 1187. The British also administered the Mandate from Jerusalem between 1921 and 1947.

Many great Gentile kings, besides the Jewish monarchs David and Solomon, have reigned over Jerusalem; such as Cyrus the Great, Alexander the Great, Constantine the Great, and Suleiman the Magnificent. Though Jerusalem is to be "trodden down of the Gentiles until the times of the Gentiles be fulfilled" (Lk 21:24), yet Jerusalem is destined to become "the city of the great king" (Ps 48:2).

The rabbis believed that Adam was created there, while others maintained that all the world was created from Jerusalem. "God started the earth from Zion," they wrote. Jewish legend says that when God said, "Let there be light," the first rays of light fell upon the Holy Land. From there it spread to illuminate the entire world. Philo said that Jerusalem is "situated in the center of the world," and just as the center of the world is Israel, and the center of Israel is Jerusalem, and the center of Jerusalem is the temple, and the center of the temple is the holy place, and the center of the holy place is the ark; in front of the holy place is the *eben hashettiyah* (foundation stone), from which the world was started. Deuteronomy 17:8 instructs opponents in a controversy to go *up* to Jerusalem for arbitration. This verse shows, said the rabbis, that the temple is higher than the rest of Eretz Israel, and that Eretz Israel is higher than all the other countries. In Jerusalem is the name of God, for the

Talmud says, "Three are called by the Name of God: Zaddikim, Messiah and Jerusalem." The Zohar even declares that there is a Jerusalem in heaven, for "the Holy One, Blessed be He, hath built a Jerusalem above in the likeness of the one below." The rabbis also believed that no person was ever stricken in Jerusalem, no person ever stumbled in Jerusalem, no fire ever broke out there, no building ever collapsed in Jerusalem. Of the ten measures of beauty which God gave to the world, the rabbis taught that nine of them were given to Jerusalem. Men are more handsome in Jerusalem, and women are more beautiful there. No scorpion or serpent ever stung in Jerusalem, no woman ever miscarried, and no man was ever injured there. No mortgage was ever foreclosed in Jerusalem, said the rabbis. Rabbi Yose said that "wherever a Jerusalemite went, they would spread out for him a soft seat, and place him on it in order to hear his wisdom."

Muslims also revere Jerusalem. They believe that if one prays in Jerusalem, he will be sure of having a succession of descendants who will also pray there. They believe that one prayer uttered in Jerusalem will outweigh a thousand prayers prayed elsewhere. If one prays in Jerusalem, he is assured of contact with a spot where an angel or a prophet has previously prayed, especially since Muslims touch the ground with their heads when they pray. When one makes a pilgrimage to Jerusalem, he is assured of merit, for seventy thousand angels pray nightly for such pilgrims, even as Allah looks down from heaven, through a door left ajar for just such purposes, upon these pilgrims. Muslims also believe that the dead will be raised and assembled in Jerusalem in order to be judged—the eight graceful arches which can be seen today situated at the heads of the eight stairways which ascend to the Dome of the Rock will hold the scales upon which the souls of men will be weighed at the end of time. The little Dome of Ascension, built in the thirteenth century A.D. upon Temple Mount, commemorates Muhammad's leap into heaven. His footprints are even yet in the sacred rock—chipped out by souvenir-hunting Crusaders—but believed by pious Muslims to be the actual indentation made by their leader's mighty leap. The sacred rock is in the center of a small but elaborate Muslim sanctuary, the Dome of the Rock, built in the late seventh century A.D.

Teddy Kollek, mayor of Jerusalem, has written:

> Archaeologists and historians have long wondered why Jerusalem should have been established where it was, and why it should have become great. It enjoys none of the physical features which favored the advancement and prosperity of other important cities in the world. It stands at the head of no great river. It overlooks no great harbor. It commands no great highway and no cross-roads. It is not close to abundant sources of water, often the major reason for establishment of a settlement, though one main natural spring offered a modest supply. It possesses no mineral riches. It is off the main trade routes. It held no strategic key to the conquest of vast areas prized by the ancient warring empires. Indeed, it was blessed with neither special economic nor topographic virtues which might explain why it should ever have become more than a small, anonymous mountain village with a fate any different from that of most contemporary villages which have long since vanished.[9]

The significance of Jerusalem is hidden in the eternal councils of God, for the Lord Himself has determined that the city will become the center of the earth—just as the medieval mapmakers felt that it should be!

Messianic Judaism has great aspirations for the city of Jerusalem. The rabbis said, "Jerusalem in days to come will ascend higher and higher until she will have reached the Throne of God." "In the future Jerusalem will become the capital of the world." "Jerusalem in the future will become a great light to all the nations." "In the future the gates of Jerusalem will reach to Damascus." How can this be? The Great Midrash on Genesis 5:7 tells us:

> Rabbi Johanan visited Rabbi Hanina and found him reading aloud Jeremiah 3:17: "At that time they shall call Jerusalem the Throne of the Lord; and all nations shall be gathered into it, to the name of the Lord, to Jerusalem." Rabbi Johanan asked: "Will it hold all nations? Will it be large enough to constitute the Throne of the Lord?" Rabbi Hanina replied: "God will say unto it: Become long, become wide, and receive within thyself all the multitudes who come."

Rabbi Simon Ben-Gamaliel declared, "All nations and all kingdoms will in the time to come gather together in the midst of Jerusalem." The Midrash also declares, "Jerusalem will be extended on all sides and the exiles will come and rest under it and it will reach the gates of Damascus." The Talmud quotes Rabbi Simon Ben-Lakish as saying, "The Holy One, Blessed be He, will in the days to come add to Jerusalem more than a thousand gardens and a thousand towers." The Midrash says, "In the future the Holy One, Blessed be He, will bring forth living waters from Jerusalem and with them heal everyone who is sick." The Midrash also says, "The Holy One, Blessed be He, will build Jerusalem of sapphire stone and these stones shall shine like the sun, and the nations will come and look upon the glory of Israel." The rabbis also predicted, "The borders of Jerusalem in time to come will be full of precious stones and pearls, and Israel will come and take their jewels from them." When Rabbi Johanan found that the Song of Solomon mentioned the "daughters of Jerusalem" three times, he identified these daughters of Jerusalem as Gentiles. He said, "In time to come God will make Jerusalem a mother-city for the whole world, as it is said, 'And I will give them to thee as daughters, though they be not of thy covenant'" (Eze 16:61).

There is little question that in Jewish literature the past glories of Jerusalem are coupled with the anticipation of a future restoration of the city to a position of world acclaim. Do the prophetic Scriptures confirm this?

When Solomon had completed the first temple, the Lord appeared to him and said, "I have hallowed this house, which thou hast built, to put my name there for ever; and mine eyes and my heart shall be there perpetually" (1 Ki 9:3). The temple is meant, but it is the city of Jerusalem which provides the environment of the temple. Jerusalem is also included in this affirmation: "Whereof the LORD said, In Jerusalem shall my name be for ever" (2 Ch 33:4). The prophet Joel says, "So shall ye know that I am the LORD your God, dwelling in Zion my holy mountain: then shall Jerusalem be holy, and there shall no strangers pass through her any more" (3:17). Micah repeats the words which are found in Isaiah, almost verbatim (cf. Is 2:2-4):

> But in the latter days it shall come to pass, that the mountain
> of the LORD's house shall be established on the top of the
> mountains, and it shall be exalted above the hills; and peoples
> shall flow unto it. And many nations shall go and say, Come
> ye, and let us go up to the mountain of the LORD, and to the
> house of the God of Jacob; and he will teach us of his ways,
> and we will walk in his paths. For out of Zion shall go forth
> the law, and the word of the LORD from Jerusalem; and he
> will judge between many peoples, and will decide concerning
> strong nations afar off: and they shall beat their swords into
> plowshares, and their spears into pruning-hooks; nation shall
> not lift up sword against nation, neither shall they learn war
> any more. . . .And I will make that which was lame a rem-
> nant, and that which was cast far off a strong nation: and
> the LORD will reign over them in mount Zion from henceforth
> even for ever (Mic 4:1-3, 7).

Jesus Himself called Jerusalem the city of the great King (Mt
5:35). He was quoting from Psalm 48:1-2: "Great is the
LORD, and greatly to be praised, In the city of our God, in his
holy mountain. Beautiful in elevation, the joy of the whole
earth, Is Mount Zion, on the sides of the north, The city of
the great King." It is from this city that the Lord Jesus Christ
will reign in glory during the Messianic age.

> Sing and rejoice, O daughter of Zion; for, lo, I come, and I
> will dwell in the midst of thee, saith the LORD. And many
> nations shall join themselves to the LORD in that day, and
> shall be my people; and I will dwell in the midst of thee, and
> thou shalt know that the LORD of hosts hath sent me unto
> thee. And the LORD shall inherit Judah as his portion in the
> holy land, and shall yet choose Jerusalem (Zec 2:10-12).

This is confirmed in such passages as:

> At that time they shall call Jerusalem the throne of the LORD;
> and all the nations shall be gathered unto it, to the name of the
> LORD, to Jerusalem: neither shall they walk any more after
> the stubbornness of their evil heart (Jer 3:17).

> Thus saith the LORD of hosts: I am jealous for Zion with great
> jealousy, and I am jealous for her with great wrath. Thus

saith the LORD: I am returned unto Zion, and will dwell in the midst of Jerusalem: and Jerusalem shall be called The city of truth; and the mountain of the LORD of hosts, The holy mountain (Zec 8:2-3).

Then the moon shall be confounded, and the sun ashamed; for the LORD of hosts will reign in mount Zion, and in Jerusalem; and before his elders shall be glory (Is 24:23).

Rabbi Gamaliel II, successor to Rabbi Johanan Ben-Zakkai, transported in his imagination and contemplating the wonders of the new earth which is to come during the Messianic age, said, "In those days women will bear children daily and trees will give forth their fruit every day!" This is not an idealistic view of heaven or eternity. The rabbis made a distinction between the eternal state and the glories of the Messianic age. For example, in the Talmud, Rabbi Johanan said, "Every prophet prophesied only for the days of the Messiah; but as for the world to come, no eye hath seen what God has prepared for those who wait for Him." The Scriptures also see a difference between the transformed earth during the reign of the Messiah and the eternal state. The latter will involve the descent of the New Jerusalem upon an earth purged by fire. However, a transformation of the physical world will occur in connection with the second coming of Christ and will primarily affect the geography of the Holy Land in preparation for the thousand-year reign of the Messiah in Israel.

The first topographical change which will occur is the altering of the Mount of Olives. The prophet Zechariah declares that this will occur when the returning Messiah's feet touch the mount:

And his feet shall stand in that day upon the mount of Olives, which is before Jerusalem on the east; and the mount of Olives shall be cleft in the midst thereof toward the east and toward the west, and there shall be a very great valley; and half of the mountain shall remove toward the north, and half of it toward the south (Zec 14:4).

The purpose of this cleavage has more to do with the closing events of the great tribulation period than it does with the Messianic reign, for it seems to provide a temporary avenue of escape for the embattled Jews in Jerusalem (cf. v. 5). However, Zechariah also indicates that this cleavage provides a new valley which will enable water to flow directly from the city of Jerusalem down to the Dead Sea (v. 8). This latter purpose has very pertinent millennial implications, for a new river will flow from the city during the Messianic age.

The second topographical change which will occur during the Messianic age is the elevation of the city of Jerusalem. Several Old Testament prophets noted this. Zechariah says that Jerusalem "shall be lifted up" (14:10). Isaiah pictures the holy city as situated on the top of a high mountain (2:2-4). He even declares that "all nations shall flow unto it" (v. 2), as his imagery defies the law of gravity! Isaiah's contemporary in the eighth century, the country preacher Micah, also concurs with this picture of exalted Jerusalem (4:1-5).

Today the Jordan river flows into the Dead Sea some twenty miles due east of the city of Jerusalem. This is not only the closest, but it is the only river in the environs of Jerusalem. However, the prophets saw another river which would issue directly from the city itself during the Messianic age. The psalmist said, "There is a river, the streams whereof make glad the city of God, The holy place of the tabernacles of the Most High" (46:4; cf. Joel 3:18). Zechariah said, "And it shall come to pass in that day, that living waters shall go out from Jerusalem; half of them toward the eastern sea [Dead Sea] and half of them toward the western sea [Mediterranean]: in summer and in winter shall it be. And the LORD shall be King over all the earth: in that day shall the LORD be one, and his name one" (14:8-9). Ezekiel said that the head of this river is the temple itself, for "Waters issued out from under the threshold of the house eastward. . . .And the waters came down from under, from the right side of the house, on the south of the altar" (47:1).

This river grows gradually deeper as it flows from the millennial temple. At first it is ankle deep (v. 3), then knee deep (v. 4), then waist deep, and finally it becomes deep enough in which to swim (v. 5). This river flows from the temple down through the wilderness of Judea into the Dead

Sea. When these healing waters pass into the Dead Sea, the sea becomes alive with aquatic life, like the Mediterranean Sea.

> Then said he unto me, These waters issue forth toward the eastern region, and shall go down into the Arabah; and they shall go toward the sea; into the sea shall the waters go which were made to issue forth; and the waters shall be healed. And it shall come to pass, that every living creature which swarmeth, in every place whither the rivers come, shall live; and there shall be a very great multitude of fish; for these waters are come thither, and the waters of the sea shall be healed, and every thing shall live whithersoever the river cometh (Eze 47:8-10).

On the banks of the river grow trees. "Now when I had returned, behold, upon the bank of the river were very many trees on the one side and on the other" (v. 7). These will afford a perpetual supply of fruit and foliage for both healing and food:

> And by the river upon the bank thereof, on this side and on that side, shall grow every tree for food, whose leaf shall not wither, neither shall the fruit thereof fail: it shall bring forth new fruit every month, because the waters thereof issue out of the sanctuary; and the fruit thereof shall be for food, and the leaf thereof for healing (v. 12).

It is interesting that the recently excavated Qumran community, near which some of the Dead Sea Scrolls were found, is located at the point where this river would naturally flow into the Dead Sea. Some scholars think that the Essenes who inhabited this community picked this spot in order to be near the river when it begins to flow from the temple during the Messianic age.

The third topographical change will be the leveling of the land around the mountain of Jerusalem. This is inferred from the description which Ezekiel gives of the redistribution of the land among the twelve tribes of Israel (48:1-29). Each tribe is given a new territory whose borders are parallel lines running due east from the Mediterranean sea.[10] The redistribution of the land has three major divisions. There are seven tribes on the north: Dan, Asher, Naphtali, Manasseh, Ephraim, Reuben, and Judah (Eze 48:1-7). On the south the land is alloted to Benjamin, Simeon, Issachar, Zebulun, and Gad (vv. 23-27). Located between these two divisions is the holy oblation (vv. 8-20). The Levites will occupy an area in the holy oblation, whose dimensions are 25,000 by 10,000 reeds. The temple and the priests will occupy another area 25,000 by 10,000 reeds, while the city's borders are 25,000 by 5,000 reeds. How long is a reed? Opinions differ. Unger suggests that a reed equals 7.2 feet, and concludes that the holy oblation would measure 34 miles square, containing about 1160 square miles of space.[11] The redistribution of the land among the tribes of Israel may represent Israel for the first time possessing all the territory that God promised to Abraham (Gen 15:18-21), especially since several of the Old Testament prophets note that the borders of Israel will be greatly enlarged during the Messianic age (Is 26:15; 33:17; Ob 17-21; Mic 7:14).

Thousands of years ago there came together on the eastern shores of the Mediterranean Sea a divinely created relationship in which the spiritual history of mankind was to find its beginning and its end. A people, a land, and a language were in confluence there. In Israel's birth the sublime destiny of mankind was manifest, for to that elect people, in the holy language, in their own land, Yahweh the covenant God of Israel, promised a Messiah who would redeem all the world from the bondage of sin. For centuries this trinity was split asunder. The people, the land, and the language were parted. The people were scattered in exile, the language all but died, and the land was taken over by aliens. Separated from each other, none of these three achieved the manifest destiny which was marked out for them from the beginning. But today, the modern State of Israel is nothing more wonderful than the reunion of the people, the language, and the land. And with this reunion the cycle of history has come full orbit. All that awaits the completion is the coming of Messiah.

Because God has ordained that eschatological events find their fulfillment in the context of Israel's resettlement in the land, the stage has now been set for the second coming of Christ. When He comes, He will reign upon the throne of David as Israel's Messiah, as well as the divine Benefactor of all redeemed mankind.

The ancient prophets of Israel have employed the *lashon kodesh*—the holy language—to depict the golden age of the Messiah's reign upon earth. The Greek of the New Testament presents this age in a graphic, but restrained way (Rev 20:1-6). Only these six verses in all the New Testament describe the millennial reign of the Lord Jesus Christ upon earth following His second coming. But what could the New Testament add—after it has identified Israel's Messiah—when the Old Testament is replete with the most majestic and incomparable descriptions of the Messianic age?

These promises are so profuse that the expositor is embarrassed at the wealth of material which is presented in the Torah, in the Writings, and in the Prophets of Israel concerning the reign of the Messiah. Hundreds of passages describe the change which will occur in the physical earth and in the animal kingdom during the age to come. The wilderness and the dry land shall be glad in that day, and the desert shall rejoice and blossom as a rose. In the wilderness water shall break out, and there shall be streams in the desert. The glowing sand will become a pool, and the thirsty ground springs of water. The wolf shall dwell with the lamb, the leopard shall lie down with the kid, the calf and the young lion shall lie together, and a little child shall lead them. The cow and the bear shall feed together, and the lion will eat straw like an ox. The little child shall play over the nest of the snake and thrust his hand into the adder's den but shall not be harmed, for these animals shall not hurt nor destroy in all the holy mountain, because the earth shall be as full of the knowledge of the Lord as the waters that cover the sea (Is 35:1, 6-7; 11:6-9).

The theocratic kingdom of the Messiah is presented in all its provisional blessings—civil, social, and economic. World chaos will cease, for the nations shall beat their swords into plowshares and their spears into pruninghooks; nation shall not lift up sword against nation, neither shall they learn war anymore (Mic 4:3). Universal peace and prosperity is held out as the only viable option for life in the Messianic age. Spiritual factors will be ideal, for not only will Satan be bound during this time, but all will worship the King in righteousness and truth. The nations shall be joyful in the house of prayer; their burnt offerings and sacrifices will be accepted upon the Lord's altar, for His house shall be called the house of prayer for all people (Is 56:7). Every day will be a holy day in the Messianic age, for from one new moon to another, and from one Sabbath to another shall all flesh come and worship before the Lord (66:23). Holiness will characterize the relationship between every man and his neighbor, for in that day shall there be upon the bells of the horses, "Holy unto the Lord"; all the pots in Jerusalem shall be like the holy vessels before the altar (Zec 14:20). Nothing shall be secular; everything shall be sanctified. Personal security will prevail, for all that threatens health and longevity will be gone. The eyes of the blind shall be opened, and the ears of the deaf shall be unstopped (Is 35:5). The ransomed of the Lord will come with singing unto Zion, and everlasting joy shall be upon their heads. They shall obtain gladness and joy, for sorrow and sighing shall flee away (v 10).

National tranquility will prevail, for all that threatens the nations in this age shall be gone. The authority of a divine *Pax Romana* will prevail, for the Messiah shall rule the earth with a rod of iron. Worship need not be encouraged, for all shall know the Lord, from the least unto the greatest (Jer 31:34), and each person shall be inspired to take the initiative in spiritual service. Joy and gladness shall ring the world, and the glory of the Messiah will cause the nations to arise and shine, for their light has now come.

Rabbi Berechiah said, "When Jacob dreamed of the ladder ascending into Heaven, he saw Babylon, Persia, Greece and Rome ascend and fall. Then God said: 'Jacob, ascend thou now.' But Jacob hesitated and asked, 'Will I not fall, O Lord, as they have fallen?' The Lord replied: 'You shall not fall.' Nevertheless, Jacob still disbelieved and was in no hurry to ascend. God then permitted other non-Jewish nations to ascend to power while Israel continued to be the victim of harsh treatment. Jacob then cried out: 'Have I lost for my descendants the chance for all time to ascend?' 'Nay,' answered God, 'in the end your people too will ascend and will not fall.'"

Three thousand years ago, the Hebrew prophets attacked the prevailing idea that war was an inevitable state of the universe. In the place of this hostile chaos which their neighbors believed to be inherent in the very nature of man, they taught the ideal: "They shall beat their swords into plowshares, and their spears into pruning-hooks; nation shall not lift up sword against nation, neither shall they learn war any more" (Is 2:4). Israel became the responsible trustee for this ideal of universal peace, along with the two other ideals which Israel conceived—individual morality and social justice. During centuries of hostile dominion by the Assyrians, the Babylonians, the Persians, the Greeks, and finally the Romans, the Jews projected the ultimate goal of a golden age of universal peace. During two thousand years of exile the ideal was not lost even when inquisition, pogroms, and genocide were determined upon them by a world hostile to these ideals and to the people who idealized them.

And for Israel in the future:

> In that day shall this song be sung in the land of Judah: We have a strong city; salvation will he appoint for walls and bulwarks. Open ye the gates, that the righteous nation which keepeth faith may enter in. Thou wilt keep him in perfect peace, whose mind is stayed on thee; because he trusteth in thee (Is 26:1-3).

And for Israel, perfect peace—shalom, shalom!

NOTES

CHAPTER ONE

1. Josephus *Wars of the Jews* 6.10.1.
2. Abraham Rabinovich, "Nineteenth Anniversary of the Destruction," *Israel*, March 1971, p. 53.
3. Dio Cassius *Roman History* 69.12-14.
4. Ibid
5. Philip Birnbaum, *A Book of Jewish Concepts*, p. 168.
6. Milton Steinberg, *As a Driven Leaf*, p. 239.
7. Yigael Yadin, *Bar Kokhba*, p. 15.
8. Andre Schwarz-Bart, *The Last of the Just*, pp. 9-10. Used by permission of Atheneum Pub. Co.
9. Both written early in the twentieth century.
10. Nahum Goldmann, *The Autobiography of Nahum Goldmann*, p. 79.
11. Max I. Dimont, *The Indestructible Jew*, pp. xvii-xviii. Used by permission of The New American Library.
12. Abba Eban, *My People*, p. 120. Used by permission of Random House, Inc.
13. Max Nordau, address at the First Zionist Congress, quoted in *The Zionist Idea*, ed. Arthur Herzberg, p. 237.
14. Isaac Peretz, quoted in *A Treasury of Jewish Quotations*, ed. Joseph Baron, p. 558.
15. Abraham Foxman, "Vilna—Story of a Ghetto," *Journal of Social Studies*, 20 (Fall-Winter, 1962).
16. Zacharias Frankel, quoted in *A Treasury of Jewish Quotations*, p. 176.
17. Isaac Peretz, quoted in ibid.
18. Eban, p. 107.
19. David Ben-Gurion, as quoted by Jean Larteguy, *The Walls of Israel*, p. 41. © 1969 by Jean Larteguy; reprinted by permission of the publisher, M. Evans and Co., New York, N.Y.
20. Alexandra Kalmykowa, quoted in *A Treasury of Jewish Quotations*, p. 234.
21. Max Dimont, *Jews, God and History*, p. 313.

CHAPTER TWO

1. Theodor Herzl, quoted in *The Zionist Idea*, ed. Arthur Herzberg, p. 220.
2. *The Zionist Idea*, p. 242.
3. Ibid., p. 372.
4. Joseph Klausner, *The Messianic Idea in Israel*, p. 9.

CHAPTER THREE

1. Josephus *Wars of the Jews* 9.1.
2. Ibid. 8.3.
3. Ibid. 9.2.
4. "Real Peace Abroad?" *U. S. News and World Report*, January 7, 1974, p.30.
5. For a series of maps showing the extent and continuity of Jewish settlements in Palestine during the long history of the second exile, see James Parkes, *A History of Palestine from 135 A.D. to Modern Times*, pp. 180-81.

CHAPTER FOUR

1. Alexander Donat, *The Holocaust Kingdom*, p. 100.
2. Sanhedrin 97b; Sukkah 45b.
3. *Encyclopedia Judaica* (Jerusalem: Keter, 1972), s.v. "Holocaust."
4. Eugene Davidson, *The Trial of the Germans*, p. 75.
5. Nora Levin, *The Holocaust*, p. 709.

6. Jacob Glatstein, Israel Knox, and Samuel Margoshes, *Anthology of Holocaust Literature* (Philadelphia: Jewish Publication Society, 1969), pp. xvii-xviii.
7. Sibylline Oracles 3.795-96; Enoch 80.2-8; 91.6-7.
8. Sanhedrin 97a.
9. Julius H. Greenstone, *The Messiah Idea in Jewish History*, p. 94.
10. Abraham of Granada, as quoted in Abba Hillel, *A History of Messianic Speculation in Israel*, p. 109.
11. Quoted in Greenstone, p. 184.
12. *Encyclopedia Judaica*, s.v. "Messiah."
13. Mordecai M. Kaplan, *The Greater Judaism in the Making*, p. 69.
14. Herman Kahn and Anthony J. Wiener, *The Year 2000*, p. 189.
15. Ibid., p. 193.
16. Howard Snyder, "A World Come Full Circle," *Christianity Today*, January 7, 1972, pp. 9-13.
17. Solomon Zeitlin, *The Rise and Fall of the Judaean State* 1.91.
18. Louis I. Newman, *The Hasidic Anthology*, pp. 301-2.
19. S. B. Unsodorfer, quoted in *Anthology of Holocaust Literature*, p. 263.

CHAPTER FIVE

1. For a magnificent critique of Toynbee's fossil theory of Israel, see Abba Eban, *Voice of Israel*, pp. 185-86.
2. Earl Raab, "American Jewry in Ferment," *Israel*, October 1972, p. 14.
3. Norman H. Snaith, *The Distinctive Ideas of the Old Testament*, p. 135.
4. Josephus *Antiquities of the Jews* 11.8.5.
5. E. B. Pusey, *The Minor Prophets* 2.404-6, gives a full list of these quotations from the Talmud, Midrash, and Zohar, indicating the almost universal opinion among Jewish expositors that the Messiah and His coming kingdom is in view in this passage.
6. Joseph Klausner, *The Messianic Idea in Israel*, p. 392.
7. Louis Ginzberg, *The Legends of the Jews*, pp. 166-67.
8. See S. R. Driver, A. Plummer, and C. A. Briggs, eds., *International Critical Commentary* (Edinburgh: T & T Clark, 1967), notes on Genesis 6.
9. Moshe Pearlman and Teddy Kolleck, *Jerusalem*, p. 12.
10. See *The Living Bible* (Wheaton: Tyndale, 1971), p. 741 for a diagram of the allotment of the land.
11. Merrill F. Unger, "The Temple Vision of Ezekiel," *Bibliotheca Sacra*, October 1948, p. 428.

A SELECTED BIBLIOGRAPHY

Adler, Bill, ed. *Israel: A Reader*. Philadelphia: Chilton, 1968.
Akiba, ben Joseph. *The Book of Formation (Sepher Yetzirah)*. New York: Ktav, 1970.
Aldouby, Zwy, and Ballinger, Jerrold. *The Shattered Silence*. New York: Coward, McCann, & Geohegan, 1971.
Allon, Yigal. *Shield of David*. New York: Random, 1970.
Anatoli, A. *Babi Yar*. New York: Farrar, Straus, & Giroux, 1970.
Anner, Zeev, and Alkoni, Yoseph. *The War 1967*. Tel Aviv: Otpaz, 1967.
Aron, Milton. *Ideas and Ideals of the Hassidim*. New York: Citadel, 1969.
Ausubel, Nathan. *The Book of Jewish Knowledge*. New York: Crown, 1964.
———. *A Treasury of Jewish Folklore*. New York: Crown, 1948.
Avineri, Sholomo, ed. *Israel and the Palestinians*. New York: St. Martin's, 1971.
Baal-Teshura, Jacob. *The Mission of Israel*. New York: Speller, 1963.
Baeck, Leo. *Judaism and Christianity*. Philadelphia: Jewish Publication Society (JPS), 1960.
———. *This People Israel*. Philadelphia: JPS, 1965.
Barer, Shlomo. *The Magic Carpet*. London: Secker & Warburg, 1952.
Baron, Joseph, ed. *A Treasury of Jewish Quotations*. New York: Crown, 1956.
Baron, Salo. *A Social and Religious History of the Jews*. 13 vols. Philadelphia: 1952.
Bar-Zohar, Michael. *Embassies In Crisis*. Englewood Cliffs, N.J.: Prentice-Hall, 1970.
Bauer, Yehuda. *Flight and Rescue*. New York: Random, 1970.
Bein, Alex. *Theodore Herzl: A Biography*. Philadelphia: JPS, 1956.

Ben-Amos, Dan, and Mintz, Jerome R. *In Praise of the Baal Shem Tov*. Bloomington, Ind.: Indiana U., 1970.

Ben-Gurion, David. *Israel:A Personal History*. Tel Aviv: Ameri. Israel Pub., 1971.

———. *The Jews in Their Land*. New York: Doubleday, 1966.

Bentwich, Norman. *For Zion's Sake*. Philadelphia: JPS, 1954.

———. *Hellenism*. Philadelphia: JPS, 1919.

Bermant, Chaim. *Troubled Eden*. New York: Basic, 1970.

Bikel, Theodore, and Podwal, Mark. *Let My People Go: A Haggadah*. New York: Darien, 1972.

Birnbaum, Philip. *A Book of Jewish Concepts*. New York: Heb. Pubns., 1964.

———. *High Holyday Prayer Book*. New York: Heb. Pubns., 1951.

———. *Prayer Book for Sabbath and Festivals*. New York: Heb. Pubns., 1964.

Bloch, Sam E. *Holocaust and Rebirth*. Tel Aviv: Bergen-Belsen, 1965.

Bondy, Ruth; Zmora, Ohad; and Bashan, Raphael. *Mission Survival*. New York: Sabra, 1968.

Brande, William. *The Midrash on Psalms*. Yale Judaica Series, vol. XIII: 1-2. New Haven, Conn.: Yale, 1959.

———. *Pesikta Rabbati*. Yale Judaica Series, vol. XVIII: 1-2. New Haven, Conn.: Yale, 1968.

Bransten, Thomas R. *Memoirs of David Ben-Gurion*. Cleveland: World, 1970.

Bridger, David. *The New Jewish Encyclopedia*. New York: Behrman, 1962.

Brilliant, Moshe. *Portrait of Israel*. New York: Amer. Heritage, 1970.

Buber, Martin. *Hasidism and Modern Man*. New York: Horizon, 1958.

———. *Tales of the Hasidim: The Early Masters*. New York: Schocken, 1947.

———. *Tales of the Hasidim: The Later Masters*. New York: Schocken, 1948.

Capa, Cornell, ed. *Israel: The Reality*, Cleveland: World, 1969.

Charel, Charles, ed. and trans. *Ramban (Nachmanides) Commentary on the Torah*. New York: Shilo, 1971.

Chesnoff, Richard; Klein, Edward; and Littell, Robert. *If Israel Lost the War*. New York: Coward-McCann, 1969.

Christman, Henry, ed. *The State Papers of Levi Eshkol*. New York: Funk & Wagnalls, 1969.

Cohen, A. *The Five Megilloth*. London: Soncino, 1971.
——. *The Minor Tractates of the Talmud*. 2 vols. London: Soncino, 1965.
Cohen, A., ed. *The Soncino Chumash*. London: Soncino, 1971.
Cohen, Israel. *Theodor Herzl: Founder of Political Zionism*. New York: Yoselott, 1959.
Cohen, Max. *They Wanted a State*. New York: House of Hillel, 1970.
Cohn, Emil. *This Immortal People*. New York: Behrman, 1945.
Cohn, Norman. *Warrant for Genocide*. New York: Harper & Row, 1967.
Collins, Larry, and Lapierre, Dominique. *O Jerusalem!* New York: Simon & Schuster, 1972.
Comay, Joan. *Ben-Gurion and the Birth of Israel*. New York: Random, 1967.
Comay, Joan, and Pearlman, Moshe. *Israel*. New York: Macmillan, 1964.
Curtis, Michael, and Chertoff, Mordecai F. *Israel: Social Structure and Change*. New Brunswick, N.J.: Transaction, 1973.
Danby, Herbert, ed. *The Mishnah*. London: Oxford U., 1933.
Davidson, Eugene. *The Trial of the Germans*. New York: Macmillan, 1966.
Davidson, Lionel. *The Menorah Men*. New York: Harper & Row, 1966.
Davis, W. Hersey, and McDowell, Edward A. *A Source Book of Interbiblical History*. Nashville: Broadman, 1948.
Dayan, Shmuel. *Pioneers In Israel*. Cleveland: World, 1961.
Dayan, Yaël. *Israel Journal: June, 1967*. New York: McGraw-Hill, 1967.
De Koven, Ralph. *A Prayer Book with Explanatory Notes*. New York: Ktav, 1965.
De Sola Pool, David. *The Traditional Prayer Book for Sabbath and Festivals*. New York: Behrman, 1960.
Dimont, Max I. *Jews, God and History*. New York: Simon & Schuster, 1964.
——. *The Indestructible Jew*. New York: Norton, 1971.
Dineir, Ben Zion. *Israel and the Diaspora*. Philadelphia: JPS, 1969.
Dio Cassius. *Roman History*. 9 vols. The Loeb Classical Library. Cambridge: Harvard U., 1914-1927.
Donat, Alexander. *The Holocaust Kingdom*. New York: Holt, Rinehart, & Winston, 1965.
Donin, Hayim Halery. *To Be a Jew*. New York: Basic, 1972.

Draper, Theodore. *Israel and World Politics*. New York: Viking, 1968.

Dyan, Moshe. *Diary of the Sinai Campaign*. New York: Harper & Row, 1965.

Eban, Abba. *My Country*. New York: Random, 1972.

———. *My People*. New York: Behrman, 1968.

———. *Voice of Israel*. New York: Horizon, 1957.

Ehrenburg, Ilya. *Post-War Years 1945-1954*. Cleveland: World, 1967.

Eisenberg, Azriel; Goodman, Hannah Grad; and Kass, Alvin. *Eyewitnesses to Jewish History from 586 BCE to 1967*. New York: Union of Amer. Heb. Cong., 1973.

Eisenberg, Azriel. *Jerusalem Eternal*. New York: Brd. Jewish Eds., 1971.

Elon, Amos. *The Israelis, Founders and Sons*. New York: Holt, Rinehart, & Winston, 1971.

Epstein, I., ed. *The Babylonian Talmud*. 18 vols. London: Soncino, 1938.

Erslin, Bernard. *The Spirit of Jewish Thought*. New York: Gosset & Dunlap, 1969.

Essrig, Harry, and Segal, Abraham. *Israel Today*. New York: Union of Amer. Heb. Cong., 1971.

Farrell, James T. *It Has Come to Pass*. New York: Herzl Press, 1958.

Finkelstein, Lewis, ed. *The Jews, Their History, Culture and Religion*. 4 vols. Philadelphia: JPS, 1949.

Flannery, Edward H. *The Anguish of the Jews*. New York: Macmillan, 1965.

Frank, Gerold. *The Deed*. New York: Simon & Schuster, 1973.

Frank, Waldo. *Bridgehead*. New York: Braziller, 1957.

Freedman, H., and Simon, Maurice, eds. *Midrash Rabbah*. 10 vols. London: Soncino, 1961.

Freehof, Solomon B. *The Responsa Literature*. Philadelphia: JPS, 1959.

Friedlander, Gerald. *Pirkê De Rabbi Eliezer*. New York: Hermon, 1965.

Friedman, Georges. *The End of the Jewish People?* New York: Doubleday, 1967.

Gabrieli, Francesco. *The Arab Revival*. New York: Random, 1961.

Gallagher, Wes, ed. *Lightning Out of the East*. New York: Associated, 1967.

Ganzfried, Solomon. *Code of Jewish Law*. Trans. Hyman E. Goldin. New York: Heb. Pub., 1961.

Garcia-Granados, Jorge. *The Birth of Israel*. New York: Knopf, 1948.

Gaster, Theodor H. *Festivals of the Jewish Year*. New York: Sloane, 1968.

Gavran, Daniel. *The End of Days*. Philadelphia: JPS, 1970.

Gerrari, Frank. *The Case for Israel*. New York: Viking, 1967.

Ginzberg, Louis. *The Legends of the Jews*. 7 vols. Philadelphia: JPS, 1968.

———. *On Jewish Law and Lore*. Philadelphia: JPS, 1955.

Glick, S. H., trans. *Agada of the Babylonian Talmud*. 5 vols. USA: Glick, 1916.

Goldberg, Nathan. *Passover Haggadah*. New York: Ktav, 1966.

Goldin, Hyman E. *A Treasury of Jewish Holidays*. New York: Twayne, 1952.

Goldmann, Nahum. *The Autobiography of Nahum Goldmann*. New York: Holt, Rinehart, & Winston, 1969.

Goodman, Philip. *The Passover Anthology*. Philadelphia: JPS, 1961.

———. *The Purim Anthology*. Philadelphia: JPS, 1952.

———. *The Rosh Hashanah Anthology*. Philadelphia: JPS, 1970.

———. *The Yom Kippur Anthology*. Philadelphia: JPS, 1971.

Gottheil, Richard. *Zionism*. Philadelphia: JPS, 1914.

Graetz, H. *Popular History of the Jews*. 6 vols. New York: Heb. Pub., 1930.

Greenstone, Julius H. *The Messiah Idea in Jewish History*. Philadelphia: 1948.

Guttmann, Julius. *Philosophies of Judaism*. New York: Holt, Rinehart, & Winston, 1964.

Halasz, Nicholas. *Captain Dreyfus*. New York: Simon & Schuster, 1955.

Helpern, Ben. *The Idea of the Jewish State*. Cambridge: Harvard U., 1969.

Herman, Simon. *Israelis and Jews*. Philadelphia: JPS, 1971.

Hershel, Abraham. *Israel: An Echo of Eternity*. New York: Farrar, Straus, & Giroux, 1969.

Hertz, J. H., ed. *The Pentateuch and Haftorahs*. London: Soncino, 1956.

Hertzberg, Arthur. *The French Enlightenment and the Jews*. Philadelphia: JPS, 1968.

Hertzberg, Arthur, ed. *The Zionist Idea*. New York: Harper & Row, 1966.

Herzl, Theodor. *The Jewish State*. New York: Amer. Zionist Emerg. Council, 1946.

Hess, Moses. *Rome and Jerusalem*. New York: Philosophical Lib., n.d.

Hillel, Abba. *A History of Messianic Speculation in Israel*. Boston: Smith, 1959.

Horowitz, George. *The Spirit of Jewish Law*. New York: Central Book, 1963.

Howe, Irving, and Gershman, Carl. *Israel, the Arabs and the Middle East*. New York: Bantam, 1972.

Huebener, Theodor, and Hermann, Carl. *This Is Israel*. New York: Philosophical Lib., 1956.

Jacobs, Paul. *Between the Rock and the Hard Place*. New York: Random, 1970.

Jewish Encyclopedia. 12 vols. New York: Ktav, n.d.

Jung, Leo. *Israel of Tomorrow*. New York: Herald Square, 1949.

Kahn, Herman, and Wiener, Anthony J. *The Year 2000*. New York: Macmillan, 1967.

Kaplan, Chaim A. *Scroll of Agony*. New York: Macmillan, 1965.

Kaplan, Mordecai. *The Greater Judaism in the Making*. New York: Reconstructionist, 1960.

Katz, Samuel. *Days of Fire*. New York: Doubleday, 1968.

Keller, Werner. *Diaspora*. New York: Harcourt, Brace, & World, 1969.

Kimche, Jon. *The Second Arab Awakening*. New York: Holt, Rinehart, & Winston, 1970.

Kimche, Jon, and Kimche, David. *A Clash of Destinies*. New York: Praeger, 1960.

Klausner, Joseph. *The Messianic Idea in Israel*. London: Allen & Unwin, 1956.

Kurzman, Dan. *Genesis 1948: The First Arab-Israeli War*. New York: New Amer. Lib., 1970.

Larteguy, Jean. *The Walls of Israel*. New York: Evans, 1969.

Laqueur, Walter. *A History of Zionism*. New York: Holt, Rinehart, & Winston, 1972.

―――. *The Road to Jerusalem*. New York: Macmillan, 1968.

―――. *The Struggle for the Middle East*. New York: Macmillan, 1969.

Learsi, Rufus. *Fulfillment: The Epic Story of Zionism*. Cleveland: Word, 1951.
———. *Israel: A History of the Jewish People*. Cleveland: World, 1949.
Leftwich, Joseph. *Israel Zangwill*. New York: Yoselott, 1957.
Levin, Meyer. *The Story of Israel*. New York: Putnam Sons, 1966.
Levin, Nora. *The Holocaust*. New York: Cromwell, 1968.
Levine, Eryatar, and Shimoni, Yaacov. *Political Dictionary of the Middle East In the 20th Century*. Jerusalem: Jerusalem Pub., 1972.
Lewis, David L. *Prisoners of Honor, the Dreyfus Affair*. New York: Morrow, 1973.
Lewisohn, Ludwig. *Theodor Herzl*. Cleveland: World, 1955.
Lipman, Eugene J. *The Mishnah: Oral Teachings of Judaism*. New York: Viking, 1970.
Lore, Kennett. *Suez: The Twice-Fought War*. New York: McGraw-Hill, 1969.
Lowenstein, Ralph L. *Bring My Sons from Far*. Cleveland: World, 1960.
Lowenthal, Marvin, ed. *The Diaries of Theodor Herzl*. New York: Dial, 1956.
Mahler, Raphael. *A History of Modern Jewry 1780-1815*. New York: Schocken, 1971.
Marcus, Jacob R. *The Rise and Destiny of the German Jew*. Cincinnati, Ohio: Union of Amer. Heb. Cong., 1934.
Meek, Theophile James. *Hebrew Origins*. New York: Harper & Row, 1960.
Meir, Golda. *A Land of Our Own*. Philadelphia: JPS, 1973.
Meyer, Isadore S. *Early History of Zionism in America*. New York: Amer. Jew. Hist. Soc., 1958.
Miller, Irving. *Israel: The Eternal Ideal*. New York: Farrar, Straus & Cudahy, 1955.
Millgram, Abraham. *Sabbath: The Day of Delight*. Philadelphia: JPS, 1959.
Minkin, Jacob S. *The Romance of Hassidism*. New York: Macmillan, 1935.
Morton, Frederick. *The Rothschilds*. New York: Atheneum, 1962.
Newman, Louis I. *The Hasidic Anthology*. New York: Schocken, 1972.
Omer, Dvorah. *Rebirth*. Philadelphia: JPS, 1972.

Parkes, James. *A History of Palestine From 135 A.D. to Modern Times*. Oxford: U. Press, 1949.

Patai, Raphael. *The Complete Diaries of Theodor Herzl*. 5 vols. New York: Herzl Press, 1960.

———. *Tents of Jacob*. Englewood Cliffs, N.J.: Prentice-Hall, 1971.

Perlman, Moshe. *The Maccabees*. New York: Macmillan, 1973.

———. *The Zealots of Masada*. New York: Scrivener, 1967.

Perlman, Moshe, and Kolleck, Teddy. *Jerusalem*. New York: Random, 1968.

Pincus, Chasya. *Come From the Four Winds*. New York: Herzl, 1970.

Price, Walter K. *The Coming Antichrist*. Chicago: Moody, 1974.

———. *Jesus' Prophetic Sermon*. Chicago: Moody, 1972.

Prittie, Terrence. *Eshkol: The Man and the Nation*. New York: Pitman, 1969.

Pusey, E. B. *The Minor Prophets*. 2 vols. Grand Rapids: Baker, 1950.

Rabinovich, Abraham. *The Battle for Jerusalem June 5-7, 1967*. Philadelphia: JPS, 1972.

Raddok, Charles. *Portrait of a People*. 3 vols. New York: Judaica, 1965.

Radin, Max. *The Jews Among the Greeks and Romans*. Philadelphia: JPS, 1915.

Raphael, Chaim. *The Walls of Jerusalem*. New York: Knopf, 1968.

Reitlinger, Gerald. *The Final Solution*. New York: Yoselott, 1968.

Rosenberger, Erwin. *Herzl as I Remember Him*. New York: Herzl Press, 1959.

Roth, Cecil. *The Passover Haggadah*. Tel-Aviv: Lewin-Epstein, n.d.

———. *A Short History of the Jewish People*. London: East & West Lib., 1959.

———. *The Standard Jewish Encyclopedia*. New York: Doubleday, 1959.

Roth, Cecil, and Wigoder, Jeffrey, eds. in chief. *Encyclopedia Judaica*. 16 vols. Jerusalem: Kater, 1972.

Rubin, Jacob A. *Partners in State Building*. New York: Diplomatic, 1969.

Sachar, Abram. *A History of the Jews*. New York: Knopf, 1966.

Sachar, Howard M. *From the Ends of the Earth.* Cleveland: World, 1964.

St. John, Robert. *Israel.* New York: Time, 1962.

Sartre, Jean-Paul. *Anti-Semite and Jew.* New York: Schocken, 1948.

Schechter, Betty. *The Dreyfus Affair.* Boston: Houghton Mifflin, 1965.

Schleunes, Carl A. *The Twisted Road to Auschwitz.* Urbana, Ill.: U. of Ill., 1970.

Schmidt, Dana A. *Armageddon in the Middle East.* New York: John Day, 1974.

Schwarz-Bart, Andre. *The Last of the Just.* New York: Athenium, 1961.

Schweid, Eliezer. *Israel at the Crossroads.* Philadelphia: JPS, 1973.

Schweitzer, Frederick. *A History of the Jews Since the First Century A.D.* New York: Macmillan, 1971.

Seidman, Hillel. *The Glory of the Jewish Holidays.* New York: Shengold, 1968.

Shapira, Avraham. *The Seventh Day.* New York: Scrivener, 1970.

Sharef, Zeev. *Three Days.* New York: Doubleday, 1962.

Shirer, William L. *The Rise and Fall of the Third Reich.* New York: Simon & Schuster, 1960.

Silverberg, Robert. *If I Forget Thee, O Jerusalem: American Jews and the State of Israel.* New York: Morrow, 1970.

Silverman, Morris, and Hillel. *Tishah B'Av Service.* Bridgeport, Conn.: Prayer Book Press, 1972.

Slater, Leonard. *The Pledge.* New York: Simon & Schuster, 1970.

Snaith, Norman. *The Distinctive Ideas of the Old Testament.* London: Epworth, 1950.

―――. *The Jews from Cyrus to Herod.* Surrey, England: Rel. Ed. Press, 1949.

Solis-Cohen, Emily. *Hanukkah: The Feast of Lights.* Philadelphia: JPS, 1960.

Solomon, Michael. *Magadan.* Princeton: Vertex, 1971.

Speer, Albert. *Inside the Third Reich.* New York: Macmillan, 1970.

Spengler, Oswald. *The Decline of the West.* Westminster, Md.: Knopf, 1945.

Sperling, Harry and Simon, Maurice. *The Zohar.* 5 vols. London: Soncino, 1956.

Steinberg, Milton. *As a Driven Leaf.* New York: Behrman, 1939.
Steiner, Jean-Francois. *Treblinka.* New York: Simon & Schuster, 1967.
Strack, Hermann L. *Introduction to the Talmud and Midrash.* New York: Atheneum, 1969.
Talmon, J. L. *Israel Among the Nations.* New York: Macmillan, 1970.
Tamarin, Alfred. *Revolt in Judea: The Road to Masada.* New York: Four Winds, 1968.
Tereth, Shabtai. *The Tanks of Tammuz.* New York: Viking, 1969.
Toynbee, Arnold. *A Study of History.* 12 vols. Oxford: U. Press, 1954-1901.
Uris, Leon. *Exodus.* New York: Doubleday, 1958.
———. *Mila 18.* New York: Doubleday, 1961.
Van Den Haag, Ernest. *The Jewish Mystique.* New York: Stein & Day, 1969.
Vilnay, Zev. *Legends of Jerusalem.* Philadelphia: JPS, 1973.
Warburg, James P. *Crosscurrents in the Middle East.* New York: Atheneum, 1968.
Weisbord, Robert G. *African Zionism.* Philadelphia: JPS, 1968.
Weizmann, Chaim. *Trial and Error.* 2 vols. Philadelphia: JPS, 1949.
Werblowsky, R.J.Z., and Wigoder, Geoffrey. *The Encyclopedia of the Jewish Religion.* New York: Holt, Rinehart & Winston, 1965.
Whiston, William, trans. *Josephus' Complete Works.* Grand Rapids: Kregel, 1960.
Wiesel, Elie. *One Generation After.* New York: Random, 1970.
———. *Souls on Fire: Portraits and Legends of Hasidic Masters.* New York,: Random, 1972.
Wolf, Lucien. *Sir Moses Montefiore.* New York: Harper, 1885.
Wouk, Herman. *This Is My God.* New York: Doubleday, 1959.
Yadin, Yigael. *Bar Kokhba.* New York: Random, 1971.
———. *The Story of Masada.* New York: Random, 1969.
Yadin, Yigael, and Harman, Abe, eds. *Israel.* New York: Doubleday, n.d.
Zeitlin, Solomon. *The Rise and Fall of the Judaean State.* 2 vols. Philadelphia, 1968.

INDEX

197